Relational Justice
Repairing the Breach

Relationships as a reform dynamic for criminal justice

In the light of widespread disillusionment with current measures to tackle crime, this book takes up a neglected theme at the heart of justice: the need to repair relationships damaged by crime, particularly those between victims and offenders. Thirteen authors have come together to explore this theme bringing personal and professional perspectives to the argument.

The essays challenge current thinking about the criminal justice system and are designed to encourage debate on the values underlying penal theory and practice. The book is aimed at informed practitioners but the Relational Justice reform dynamic will be of interest to all people who are concerned about crime and responses to it.

Relational Justice
Repairing the Breach

Edited by Jonathan Burnside and Nicola Baker

Foreword by Lord Woolf

WATERSIDE PRESS

Relational Justice
Repairing the Breach

Published 1994 by
WATERSIDE   PRESS
Domum Road
Winchester SO23 9NN
Telephone or Fax 0962 855567

ISBN Paperback 1 872870 22 8

Printing and binding Antony Rowe Ltd, Chippenham

Cover design John Good Holbrook Ltd, Coventry

Relational Justice
Repairing the Breach

Contributors

Nicola Baker
Co-ordinator, Jubilee Policy Group

Professor Anthony Bottoms
Wolfson Professor of Criminology, University of Cambridge and Director, Institute of Criminology

Jonathan Burnside
Researcher, Jubilee Policy Group

His Honour Judge Christopher Compston
Circuit Judge

Dr Andrew Coyle
Governor, H M Prison, Brixton

Professor Christie Davies
Professor of Sociology and Head of the Department of Sociology, University of Reading

David Faulkner CB
Fellow, St John's College, Oxford

John Harding
Chief Probation Officer, Inner London Probation Service

His Honour Judge FWM McElrea
District Court Judge, Auckland, New Zealand

Roger Shaw
Chief Probation Officer, Powys Probation Service

Dr Michael Schluter
Director, Jubilee Policy Group

Christopher Townsend
Solicitor

Peter Walker
Director, Prison Fellowship England and Wales

Biographical Details

Nicola Baker is the Co-ordinator of the Jubilee Policy Group, the research arm of the Jubilee Centre in Cambridge. The Policy Group is concerned to review public policy issues from a Christian perspective and to develop new approaches to contemporary social and economic questions. She graduated in history at Oxford University and has previously worked in political research, public relations and international finance.

Professor Anthony Bottoms is Wolfson Professor of Criminology at the University of Cambridge and a Fellow of Fitzwilliam College. He has been Director of the Institute of Criminology, Cambridge since 1984. His main research interests lie in the fields of criminal justice policy and environmental criminology and he has conducted empirical research studies on a wide range of topics including imprisonment, non-custodial penalties, crime prevention and crime and housing. His publications include *The Urban Criminal* (1976), *Defendants in the Criminal Process* (1976), *The Coming Penal Crisis* (1980), *Problems of Long-Term Imprisonment* (1987) and *Intermediate Treatment and Juvenile Justice* (1990). He is currently completing a major evaluation of Intermediate Treatment for the Department of Health.

Jonathan Burnside read law at Trinity College, Cambridge and took an M Phil at the Institute of Criminology, Cambridge. He has been the principal researcher with the Jubilee Policy Group on the Relational Justice project since 1992. *Relational Justice: A reform dynamic for criminal justice* (1994) summarises the policy implications of the research project.

His Honour Judge Christopher Compston has been a Circuit Judge since 1986 sitting on criminal, civil and family cases as well as being a President of Mental Health Review Tribunals. He is the author of *Recovering from Divorce* (1993).

Dr **Andrew Coyle** has worked in the Prison Service for over 20 years. He has been Governor of Greenock, Peterhead and Shotts prisons and since 1991 has been Governor of Brixton prison. He is an associate member of the Centre for Criminology, University of Edinburgh and chairman of the Institute for the Study and Treatment of Delinquency. He has visited prison systems in Western Europe, Eastern Europe, Asia, Africa, North America and the Caribbean. His latest book is *The Prisons We Deserve* (1994).

Professor Christie Davies is Professor of Sociology and Head of the Department of Sociology at the University of Reading. He has published widely and his books include: *Wrongful Imprisonment: Mistaken Convictions and their Consequences* (1973), *Permissive Britain: Social Change in the Sixties and Seventies* (1975), *Censorship and Obscenity* (as joint editor, 1978) and *Ethnic Humour Around the World: a comparative analysis* (1990).

David Faulkner CB is a Fellow of St John's College, Oxford and a Senior Research Associate at the Oxford Centre for Criminological Research. He served in the Home Office from 1959 until 1992, becoming Deputy Secretary in charge of the Criminal Research and Statistics Department in 1982 and Principal Establishments Officer in 1990.

John Harding is Chief Probation Officer, Inner London Probation Service having previously been Chief Probation Officer for Hampshire, where he pioneered integrated social services. He is chair of the Association of Chief Officers of Probation Young Offenders Committee and has taken a lead role in negotiations with the Home Office and Department of Health on legislative and social policy issues concerning young offenders. He is an Associate Fellow of the Mannhiem Centre, London School of Economics, a visiting lecturer at Tokyo Far East Asia Institute (United Nations) and has published widely including as a contributor to *Paying Back: Twenty Years of Community Service* (1993), *Criminal Justice In Transition* (1994) and *The Youth Court One Year Onwards* (1994).

His Honour Judge FWM McElrea is a District Court Judge in Auckland, New Zealand and lecturer in criminal law, University of Auckland. He has reflected extensively on the radical changes which new legislation has brought to the New Zealand criminal justice system. He is joint editor of *The Youth Court in New Zealand: A New Model of Justice* (1993).

Dr Michael Schluter is the founder and Director of the Jubilee Centre in Cambridge which he set up in 1983 to develop responses to public policy issues from a Christian perspective. He trained as an economist and worked in East Africa with the World Bank and the International Food Policy Research Institute. He is joint author of *The R-Factor* (1993), which advocates a relational approach to public policy, and has set up the Relationships Foundation to pursue the application of relational thinking.

Roger Shaw is Chief Probation Officer of Powys in mid-Wales. He was previously an HM Inspector of Probation and a Teaching and Research Fellow at the Institute of Criminology, Cambridge University. He has researched the unintended consequences of imprisonment, particularly upon prisoners' children, and the supervision of dangerous offenders in the community. He is the author of several books on criminal justice, including *Prisoners' Children: What are the issues?* (1992).

Christopher Townsend is a Solicitor practising in the City of London and has been closely involved with the Relational Justice Project. This involvement began during two years spent as a Researcher with the Jubilee Policy Group. His research, other than that relating to criminal justice, has concerned biblical and theological issues relevant to the development of the work of the Jubilee Centre.

Peter Walker is the Executive Director of Prison Fellowship England and Wales, a Christian ministry to prisoners, ex-prisoners and their families. Previously, he worked in the City of London Stock Exchange. Prison Fellowship has partnered the Jubilee Policy Group throughout the Relational Justice project.

Relational Justice
Repairing the Breach

Contents

Acknowledgements

It has certainly been true that a book which reviews the relational implications of criminal justice has involved the development of many relationships.

As relative newcomers to the field of penal reform, one of our immediate impressions was that few opportunities exist which encourage the different parts of the criminal justice process to come together on a common platform. Our intention has been that this book, and the Relational Justice project as a whole, should provide one such opportunity.

Therefore, our foremost thanks go to our fellow contributors who have been willing to pave the way and lend their professional and personal insights towards the development of a penal process which sees the repair of relationships damaged by crime as a goal of the criminal justice system.

It has been our concern throughout the Relational Justice project to balance theory with practice and policy with principle. Thus, a range of disciplines and expertise has been brought to bear on this project. From the outset, the Jubilee Policy Group has benefited significantly from its proximity to the University of Cambridge Institute of Criminology. Without the personal encouragement of and constructive criticism from several of its members, we should not have had the courage to launch into the choppy waters of penology.

Justice issues inevitably raise questions of philosophy and indeed of theology. Our thinking has been guided and inspired by many conversations with those who have charted this course ahead of us. In particular, we are grateful to the Rev Dr Nicholas Sagovsky, Dean of Clare College, Cambridge.

Gratitude is also due to members of the project's steering group whose breadth of experience has added much towards assessing the practical and policy implications of the Relational Justice approach. Participating on the steering group were Kimmett Edgar, NACRO; Abi Griffin, Youth Crime Officer; Mark Halsey, barrister-at-law; the Rev Michael Hensman, former HM Assistant Chief Inspector of Probation; Guy Hordern JP; David Jones OBE, former Magistrates' Courts Adviser, Lord Chancellor's Department; David Neal, HM Prison Service; Mike Rees, Surrey Probation Service; Monseigneur Peter Walker, Prison Fellowship England and Wales and Monseigneur Peter Wilkinson, HM Prison Service Chaplaincy.

We also acknowledge with thanks the financial support of The Relationships Foundation, together with that of a number of individual private donors, without whose commitment over the three years, this project would not have been possible.

Finally, we would like to acknowledge how indebted we are to Bryan Gibson at Waterside Press. We have greatly enjoyed working with him on this publication.

Jonathan Burnside
Nicola Baker   November 1994

Foreword

There could not be a more appropriate time to publish this extremely important book. Throughout the developed world governments are searching for ways in which to stem what is perceived to be a tidal wave of anti-social behaviour. Their citizens are clamouring for protection. The response of governments is usually to give way to the demands for longer and more punitive punishments. Experience has demonstrated that this, far from being a cure, is not even a short term palliative.

The message which this book provides is that there could be an alternative approach which would stem or just possibly turn the tide. The approach involves identifying and seeking to tackle one of the major underlying causes of the breakdown of social behaviour. That cause is one which I have no hesitation in accepting exists. It is the total or partial failure of a series of relationships—the relationships which should exist among and between individuals, communities and institutions.

In the case of prisons, when Judge Tumim and I were involved in writing our Report we were convinced that the principle problem to which we had to find a solution was the unsatisfactory state of the relationships within the prison system. There was a lack of satisfactory relations between prisoner and prisoner, prisoner and prison officer, prison officer and governor, governor and headquarters and the prison system and the other agencies of the criminal justice system. This was a substantial cause of the unstable and sorry state of our prisons. There was also the problem that the lack of satisfactory relationships was accompanied by injustice. Prisoners frequently had cause for believing that justice stopped at the prison gates. The indications are that the recommendations we made have alleviated these problems in many prisons. Relations and justice have improved. It is still my hope that our recommendations will eventually play a part in reducing the deplorable amount of re-offending by those who are released from prison. As Judge Tumim wrote to the Jubilee Policy Group about this book: perhaps like '. . . Moliere who found he had been speaking prose all his life without knowing it. It seems that (he and I) have been preaching Relational Justice without knowing it, and our report is to become perhaps a Relational text book!'

However, what is occuring within our prisons forms only a small part of the scope of this book. Although one of the contributors is among our most enlightened prison governors, the others have distinguished records in many fields. They include experienced judges, criminologists, sociologists and probation officers. They examine what is wrong in our society across the board from different standpoints and their reasoning and conclusions do not always coincide. Their solutions are far from being identical. Nonetheless, collectively they produce the base on which David Faulkner, with his unique knowledge of the criminal justice system, can build a convincing case for a fresh approach—based upon *Relational Justice*. It is a radical new approach about which any one with any concern about our criminal justice system needs to be aware. The recommendations with which the book concludes are refreshingly simple but collectively they could be the 'radical new approach' which is needed. The Jubilee Policy Group and each of the contributors are to be warmly congratulated on what this book achieves.

Lord Woolf   November 1994

Introduction

1 What Is Relational Justice?
Michael Schluter

CHAPTER 1

What Is Relational Justice?

Michael Schluter

The classic cause of nervous breakdown is mounting pressure over a period of time coupled with a simultaneous decline in the ability of the person to handle the problems. Eventually, the psyche reaches breaking-point, often with tragic results. Are we approaching a 'nervous breakdown' in our criminal justice system?

The gathering storm

The signs are ominous. No-one will dispute the evidence of growing levels of crime in British society as a long-term trend. For one year alone, 1991, the *rise* in recorded crime was greater than the total level of crime in 1950[1]. Even this does not tell the whole story. Certain categories of crime are consistently under-reported. For example, shoplifting is now so prevalent that whereas in 1950 the police would generally be called so that a crime could be recorded, today retailers no longer bother as cases are so commonplace. The proportion of crimes which reach court and result in a conviction is about two per cent[2]. So the prison system represents no more than the tip of the iceberg in terms of the numbers involved in crime.

The effects of crime are far-reaching. Not least is the fear of violence which affects many more people than simply past victims. When Rachel Nickell was murdered on Wimbledon Common in 1992, many women thought again about walking their dogs in London, even in broad daylight. Motorists are generally unwilling to give hitchhikers lifts owing to a relatively small number of incidents where drivers have been attacked. What mother now feels that it is safe to leave her child in the pram outside the corner shop while she drops in for a loaf of bread?

At the same time our ability to deal with crime is declining. Once described as 'a practice without a policy'[3], credence has been afforded by criminal justice policy-makers to imprisonment as a solution. Prison appears to be ineffective either as a deterrent or as a means of reform. Home Office research shows a reconviction rate of nearly 70 per cent within four years for male offenders and of 82 per cent for those under 21.[4] We need to escape the paradox of imprisonment being increasingly condemned and yet increasingly used. Yet if prison is not the solution to growing rates of crime, it seems that other court dispositions such as community sentences have yet to become sufficiently acceptable to the public for it to be said that these can provide the answer.

So is the criminal justice system nearing a crisis similar in character to nervous breakdown? Or is there a way to narrow the gap between the scale of the problem and the efficacy of the response? Such a means must touch not just responses but causes, not the procedures of justice but its purpose, not institutions but individuals, not only the mind but also the heart.

The prevailing social ethos

In the decade to 1994 the prevailing political *zeitgeist* has sought the welfare of society through an emphasis on personal freedom and responsibility. The assumption has been that economic growth is the key. Not only does it make everyone better off financially but it establishes a framework within which all people may achieve personal fulfilment provided that they—and everyone else—abide by the rules. In commerce and finance, the goal has been to deregulate markets so as to increase freedom and opportunity for the enterprising and to increase choice for the consumer. Professor Elliot Currie has drawn attention to the way in which the United Kingdom has evolved from a market economy into a market society,[5] defined as one in which the pursuit of private gain has become the guiding principle for all areas of social life, not merely economic organization.

In the public services, the new ethos is epitomised by performance-related pay, new procedures for contracting out services, and tough financial performance indicators. Success is defined largely in financial terms even for the so-called 'service sectors' delivering education, health and welfare. For the Department of Social Security, beneficiaries have become 'customers', benefits have become 'products' and local offices have been tuned to provide 'one-stop shopping' for those on welfare. While few would question the need to make public services thoroughly cost-effective, it is always disturbing when means are transmuted into ends.

The values of materialism and individualism in contemporary Britain have even started to influence the way in which prisons are run. The 'market' becomes the invisible but controlling hand behind the way that new institutions are designed and offenders are treated. To take an example, if it is cheaper to have prisoners collect their food and eat in their cells rather than in a communal dining hall—because less guards are required—the market will dictate that food is to be eaten alone. It helps to ensure minimum cost per day per prisoner. There is no room in this conceptual framework for considerations of long-term mental health, communication skills, or the likely impact on a prisoner's relational well-being. There is a real danger that privatised prisons could become, in effect, down-market, fenced-in hotels or perhaps, in the future, zoos.

Crime and criminal justice are inevitably a product of the society we choose to create. What kind of society do we want? One option is undoubtedly to continue to place the emphasis on unfettered individual freedom. However, this absence of community creates conditions in which crime spreads like an epidemic. Ironically, then, the result of such a pursuit of freedom will be 'fortress Britain', where individuals who are excluded from, or who opt out of, the material bonanza are kept under control by surveillance cameras, electronic tagging and prison walls. The contributors to this book would like to find a better way forward.

Why think Relationally?

An antidote to this largely materialist perspective on the world would be a political philosophy which has as its starting point the centrality of human relationships, for it is in relationships that we define our identity and recognise our well-being. A good illustration is found in the film *Dances With Wolves*, where the hero—a cavalry officer in the American Civil War—finds himself caught up with a group of native Indians. Twice he comments that the experience of living in the close community of Indian tribal society has enabled him to 'find himself'. It is a truism to say it is only in and through relationships that our characters can express themselves. To live entirely alone is to lose one's humanity.

Not only self-understanding but also a sense of purpose, fulfilment and happiness come from our relationships. Multi-disciplinary research has established the wide range of areas in which stable and committed relationships contribute to the well-being of adults and children alike. Close, long-term relationships, whether with family or friends, play a crucial role in enabling individuals to enjoy good health, to achieve career goals and to cope with the difficulties encountered in old age.[6] For children, long-term stable relationships are the key to learning to communicate, in having the confidence to explore the world when young and to develop relationships with peers. The most socially competent children are generally those with secure attachments to their parents.[7]

Moral development also appears to be linked to the quality of relationships formed in childhood. Sympathy for strangers is a by-product of sympathy for one's kin. Family relationships comprise the natural forum within which each individual learns to balance his or her interests against those of the group. They enable the individual to learn to hold in balance choice (my freedom to do as I wish) and obligation (my responsibility towards others). Such individual self-understanding is the bedrock on which public order is built, and is the foundation of the criminal justice system, and it depends almost entirely on the stability of relationships and individual experiences in childhood.

At the opposite extreme, research shows that inadequate or absent parent-child relationships are associated with juvenile delinquency, violence and a range of psychological disorders including schizophrenia, eating disorders, adolescent depression and difficulty in developing social relationships. Children brought up in care, or in some adoption situations, more often have difficulty in developing relationships in later years except where the adoption was early in the child's life or where the surrogate parents have had a long-term, committed, stable relationship with the child. The effect of divorce is often insecure relationships at home with feelings of rejection in the child, or feelings of deprivation; this can then result in consequential lower self-esteem, lower social competence and, in boys especially, non-compliant behaviour.[8]

What many people have failed to appreciate is that the attitudes held in domestic relationships, and the importance that we attach to them, is determined not just by what happens in our private lives, but by the pattern of relationships in places of work, in national politics and in a host of other public institutions. The business world, for example, can be understood in terms of relationships—between employer and employee, buyer and supplier, salesperson and customer. These relationships are governed in part by the ethos of the institution, which is in turn influenced by the wider pattern of social values, as well as the personality and background of, the individuals involved. The business schools in recent years have attributed business growth and success increasingly to relational factors.[9]

What is true in business is also true in other areas of public life. The key to understanding changes within and between organizations often lies in the relational dimension. An institution like a hospital can be analysed in terms of patterns of internal relationships among patients and various categories of staff, and external relationships with government departments, commercial suppliers, and a host of other bodies. In each case there are interactions between individuals and these are governed by both formal procedures and unwritten rules.

The shift towards 'the market' in the ethos of public institutions—with the strong priority given to material considerations—is likely to have had an influence in the private lives of those who work in them or are touched by them. If consistently driven at work to give priority to cost factors over human welfare considerations, it would be easy to adopt the same attitude in the domestic environment. The pressure to achieve material success in business can lead to little time for relationships at home, just as a breakdown of relationships at home will affect performance at work. Relationships at work and at home are bound to overlap and to influence one another.

Relationships and duty

It is the relationships that we experience in both public and private life which replenish social resources of commitment and constraint and make us willing to fulfil our obligations. Where relationships within a society or community are becoming less 'close', one would expect a weakened sense of duty towards other people. The relational thesis is that a break up of relational bonding in society has weakened our sense of duty, or obligation.[10]

A person's sense of obligation to a neighbour is generally in direct proportion to how well they know that person. In the Netherlands in the summer of 1993, a girl aged nine drowned in a lake with several hundred people watching, yet no-one dived in to help her. It was all recorded by a man with a video camera, and his film was then used in a television news programme. Why did no-one take action to help the girl? The reason seems to lie in a lack of relational 'proximity' or 'closeness' in society generally. When people do not know a person in trouble, they do not feel an obligation to get involved.

The impact of this lack of a sense of 'relational proximity', which causes an absence of community involvement and responsibility can be seen over and again in reports in the press or by the media of criminal acts. A woman is dragged screaming from a bus queue to be raped and murdered, and nobody intervenes. A woman is murdered over a half hour period at the bottom of two tower blocks, repeatedly calling for help, with over a hundred people watching from their windows. Nobody goes to help; nobody even calls the police.

To understand this absence of 'relational proximity', it is helpful to explore its component parts. What is it that results in people being 'close' to each other, in having empathy with their neighbours' needs and situations? In *The R-Factor*, five dimensions are set out which provide a basis or framework for good relationships.[11] These are:

(a) Directness —the ideal that people should meet as far as possible *face-to-face* rather than having contact through a third party, or through impersonal media.

(b) Continuity—that people should meet frequently, regularly and over a sustained period of time.

(c) Multiplexity—that people should have contact in more than one role or context, so that they can see how people respond in different situations.

(d) Parity—that people should meet as equals, not in terms of role or status but in terms of their sense of personal worth or value.

(e) Commonality—that people should have as far as possible common purpose, and common experience, as these help to cement relationships.

Each of these aspects of relationship, when present, contribute towards getting to know a person better, having a common bonding, developing a sense of mutual obligation. They contribute to mutual empathy, although not necessarily to intimacy. Each of them has been affected by major social trends since 1945. This is considered below.

There is one main argument commonly deployed against the relational thesis that closeness of relationship benefits all parties, and in particular children. This is the case of marriage. Here is an arrangement where two people live in the closest proximity to one another, with every advantage of intimacy in their relationship, and yet we see so many of these relationships break down irretrievably. Why?

In many cases it is a matter of personality, incompatibility, misunderstanding or just plain bad-temper or pig-headedness. However, the reason may also be found in the social environment. For example, the reason for high divorce rates may lie in part in financial pressures emanating from debt and unemployment. A couple may find themselves relationally isolated, with few close friends, neighbours and relatives to provide a framework of supportive relationships. Sociologists use the term 'implosion' to describe what happens when a violent argument can find no outlet or mediation outside the home. More expectation has been placed on the marriage or home situation than the parties are able to bear. This may help to explain the extraordinarily high incidence of violence which occurs in a domestic context.

Social trends since 1945
A number of major trends in economic and political life have a bearing on how British society has changed since 1945. Four of these trends are considered briefly below:

Technology
What effect has technology had upon the way we conduct our relationships? Modern telephone technology and motor transport allow closer contact between geographically separated family and friends than was the case with previous generations. On the other hand, such developments can result in less face-to-face contact. When we collect money from the bank eg we now use a cashpoint instead of speaking to a cashier. The government plans to distribute pensions by cheque through the post rather than through the local post office. Television inevitably results in fewer conversation-based family meals in the home, whereas the

phenomenon of households equipped with several television sets reduces the opportunity for shared experiences yet further. Computer games involve less face-to-face encounters between friends than the street games of old such as 'tag' and 'hopscotch'. The impact of technology is complex: much depends on how it is used at both institutional and individual levels.

Mobility
Increasing mobility has been a feature of Western societies since 1945. These are not the great waves of long-term migration, where whole villages or even larger communities moved *en masse*. Rather, it is the mobility of nuclear families or single people, where movement resembles an electron dance. There is a Russian proverb which states: 'To know a man intimately, one must eat several bushels of salt with him.' As salt is consumed in very small amounts at each meal, this points to the length of time people need to spend with each other in order to establish intimacy. Mobility is one factor inhibiting such prolonged acquaintance. Nonetheless, in its defence, it may, perhaps, be said to have helped to open up relationships in British society by contributing to a breakdown of class barriers.

Size of institutions
Another change since 1945 has been the growth in the size of public institutions, whether hospitals, schools, companies or prisons. This has helped to keep down unit costs and has allowed the introduction of technology which would have been uneconomic in smaller organizations. However, the relational consequences of greater size are often negative. Generally, the larger the organisation the less face-to-face contact a person will have with a specific colleague and the more hierarchical the entire structure will be. A greater number of contacts takes the place of fewer, deeper relationships. While this can offer a *greater sense* of personal freedom, it can also lead to a decreased sense of obligation and loyalty.

The role of government
Another characteristic of the modern day is the way in which life is touched or even controlled by government. The state has increased its role in the provision of health, education and welfare, with benefits in terms of fairness and universal coverage. In 1910 the entire government share of total spending in the economy was still around ten per cent; today it is close to 50 per cent. At the same time, there has been a shift from local to central government. As recently as 1979 the proportion of a local authority budget which was set and raised locally amounted to 57 per cent: today the figure is 18 per cent.[12] How have these changes affected the way people relate to each other? Arguably, one consequence has been to remove responsibility for decision-making from families and local councils, thereby removing an

important source of common interest and bonding. Could the reduced *role* of the family and locality be connected with the evident lack of commitment people feel towards other family members and neighbours? Could this be connected, indirectly, with the growth of crime?

This brief survey of social trends since 1945 is intended to do no more than illustrate the way in which a number of factors in the external environment and in public life are having a major impact on relationships in the home and neighbourhood. Since, in the view of the contributors to this work, the relational context provides helpful insights into undertsanding and responding to crime, these changes have great significance for the criminal justice system. At the same time, the changing social environment should provide an additional impetus for a re-examination of the criminal justice system itself to assess its impact on relationships in both public and private life.

Thinking Relationally about justice

The implications of Relational thinking are far reaching. Bringing a relational perspective to bear upon the problems raised by the criminal justice system may represent a radical departure. This perspective we have termed 'Relational Justice'.

One of the foundations of this new approach is to regard crime primarily as a breakdown in relationships; even in those cases where the offender does not personally know the victim, a relationship can be said to exist by virtue of their being citizens together, bound together by rules governing social behaviour. Crime is only secondarily to be regarded as an offence against the state and its laws.

The relational damage of a crime occurs first and foremost at the level of the individuals immediately concerned—the offender and the victim. However, other relationships are also affected, including the offender's relationship with his or her family, that of the victim with his or her family, and that of the offender's family and the local community. In addition, where a crime induces fear in a neighbourhood, the knock-on effects in terms of relationships may be widespread. It is like a stone going through a spider's web and which breaches a whole nexus of interwoven relationships. It is a breach that demands attention. How might it be repaired?

Empirical research highlights how weak relationships in the family and in the locality are a significant factor in seeking to understand the causes of crime. David Farrington has traced statistically significant links between 'cold' family relationships and anti-social behaviour, a rather wider term than crime.[13] This is because poor parenting results in an absence of internalised norms and a lack of understanding as to how other people feel and react. He also argues that an absence of family and community

24

bonding increases the likelihood that anti-social feelings in an individual will be translated into offending behaviour. This is because where concern by people for one another is weak, there are good opportunities to commit crimes, and because factors like drug addiction, unemployment and drinking which lead to crime are more likely to be present.

John Braithwaite, an Australian criminologist, has argued that weak relationships in the family and the community also inhibit our ability to punish effectively.[14] He argues that punishment should shame the wrongdoer concerned and bring home to him the reality of his or her wrong-doing. But punishment is not an end in itself: it normally has in view the restoration of the individual who is punished. Braithwaite contends that shaming, at its most effective, helps to reintegrate the offender into the community and it is counter-productive when it results in stigmatisation. Reintegrative shaming is disapproval dispensed within an ongoing relationship with the offender that is based on respect. It is shaming which focuses on the evil of the deed rather than on the offender as irredeemably evil. Stigmatisation, by contrast, is shaming where bonds of respect with the offender are not sustained. The result is to create outcasts for whom criminality has become a master-status trait that drives out all other identities.

This analysis is helpful in understanding the response to a 14-year-old delinquent who took to hiding in a housing estate ventilation shaft when the police were looking for him. He was quickly dubbed 'Ratboy' by the national press. Only his mother, it seemed, could hang onto who he really was, 'He's not a rat. He's my son'.[15]

However, it is hard to be shamed unless there are people whose opinions the person being shamed cares about. Strong relationships are essential to effective shaming. So it is hard to achieve 'reintegrative shaming' today when, so often, we know people in only one social role. The prison system exacerbates the isolation of the offender from both his family and the locality, further reducing any prospect of reintegrative shaming for the future.

Relational Justice as a reform dynamic

Thinking relationally has significant implications for the justice system in practice. Any institution or situation can be analysed, with greater or lesser relevance, from a financial, environmental or educational point of view. So, too, can they be explored from a relational perspective. In the area of criminal justice, a relational analysis will include the role of the police, the way the courts operate, the forms of punishment used and the priorities accorded to both prevention and offender reintegration. But can Relational Justice give better answers to these pressing problems?

25

The contributors to this work explore the potential of Relational Justice as a reform dynamic, bringing their specialisms in different parts of the criminal justice process to bear so as to demonstrate the relevance of the concept to their own particular sphere. The aim is to provide a general overview of the application and applicability of Relational Justice—and to provide a basis for the reader to make his or her own assessment of its usefulness.

In *Chapter 2, Crime and the Rise and Decline of a Relational Society*, Christie Davies examines the validity of the relational thesis as a way of understanding why crime diminished so rapidly and remarkably at the end of the last century. Jonathan Burnside explores the conceptual tensions that arise from juxtaposing 'justice' and 'relationships' in *Chapter 3, Tension and Tradition in the Pursuit of Justice*. He argues that an ongoing dialectic between the two parts of Relational Justice is necessary. In regarding justice as a community responsibility with community obligations, he suggests that justice is only to be found within a community of just people. This appears to raise the further question of whether a society can expect to secure criminal justice if it lacks underlying social justice and economic justice. In *Chapter 4, Avoiding Injustice, Promoting Legitimacy and Relationships*, Tony Bottoms brings to bear the perspective of the criminologist.

A call to reappraise the part played by mediation and reparation within criminal justice is made by Nicola Baker in *Chapter 5, Mediation, Reparation and Justice*. A reassessment of the victim's role is also made in *Chapter 7, Justice in the Community: The New Zealand Experience*, where Judge Fred McElrea describes what would seem to be exciting developments towards a new model for sentencing, the 'Family Group Conference', in his country. Concern is expressed by Judge Christopher Compston in *Chapter 6, Local Justice: A Personal View* that conventions of local representation in justice are on the wane. These conventions, which have an underlying relational purpose, should be preserved and fostered, he argues.

The need for alternatives to the most 'anti-relational' of punishments—imprisonment (and other forms of custody)—is discussed in *Chapter 8, Youth Crime: A Relational Perspective* by John Harding and from a neglected perspective in *Chapter 9, Prisoners' Children: A Sympton of Our Failing Justice System*, by Roger Shaw. Further research is needed into the effectiveness of these alternatives. Dr Andrew Coyle writes in *Chapter 10, My Brother's Keeper: Relationships in Prison* about the kind of efforts which can make existing prison regimes more tolerable.

In *Chapter 11, Believing In Justice*, Christopher Townsend examines the concept of Relational Justice in the light of three major religious belief systems: Judaism, Christianity and Islam. The chapter provides a preliminary exploration of the extent of their compatibility with ideas which underpin Relational Justice. The human dynamics of the day-to-day caring for and control of offenders is explored in a personal view by Peter Walker in *Chapter 12, Repairing the Breach: A Personal Motivation.*

In the final chapter, *Relational Justice: A Dynamic for Reform*, David Faulkner reflects on the foregoing contributions and offers his perspective, as a former Home Office civil servant, on the policy implications of the relational approach. He argues that the time is ripe to examine how far the criminal justice system measures up to relational as well as efficiency criteria.

Crime can be both a crisis and an opportunity for society at large. As Emile Durkheim has argued, crime can be a focus and stimulus for the creation of new rules and thus for socialisation and the integration of society. It is one of the contentions of this volume that crime can and should be treated as a challenge and an opportunity for the formation of new and stronger relationships.

There is an urgent need for a reappraisal of the future of the criminal justice system. It is to stimulate open discussion and to make a contribution to the present debate that the authors offer this volume.

Notes

[1] Home Office Prison Statistics, England and Wales (London: HMSO, 1994).

[2] Information on the Criminal Justice System in England and Wales, Digest 2 (London: Home Office Research and Statistics Department, 1993)

[3] A Speller, *Breaking Out*, (London: Hodder & Stoughton, 1986).

[4] Quoted in *The Guardian*, 24 June 1994.

[5] Cited in R Kelly, 'The invisible hand behind the inexorable increase in the rate of crime'. *The Guardian*, (1 September 1993).

[6] For a summary of the evidence, from psychology and the social sciences, see E Watt, 'For Better or for Worse: The Case for Long-Term Commitment in Family Relationships' (Cambridge: Jubilee Centre, 1994).

[7] *Ibid.*

[8] *Ibid.*

[9] For evidence of this, see M Schluter and D Lee, *The R-Factor* (London: Hodder and Stoughton, 1993), pp 219-33.

[10] *Ibid.*

[11] M Schluter and D Lee, *op cit*, ch 3.

[12] *Finance, General and Rating Statistics, 1978-9* (CIPFA, London, July 1978) & *Councillor's Guide to Local Government Finance*, 92nd ed (CIPFA, London, July 1992).

[13] D P Farrington, *The Challenge of Teenage Antisocial Behaviour* Unpublished paper prepared for Marbach Castle conference on Youth in the Year 2000 (1993), p 33.

[14] J Braithwaite, *Crime, Shame and Reintegration* (Cambridge: Cambridge University Press, 1989).

[15] 'Profile: A 14 year-old becomes a byword for trouble.' *The Independent*, 9 October 1993.

Part I

Relational Responses to Crime and Society

2 Crime and the Rise and Decline of a Relational Society
Christie Davies

3 Tension and Tradition in the Pursuit of Justice
Jonathan Burnside

4 Avoiding Injustice, Promoting Legitimacy and Relationships
Anthony Bottoms

CHAPTER 2

Crime and the Rise and Decline of a Relational Society

Christie Davies

It seems probable and plausible that there is a link between the marked rise in crime that has taken place in Britain in the last forty years and the change in the quality of relationships between individuals. This change is from encounter relationships involving personal contact, closeness and continuity to contingent relationships that are brief, distant and have a single, narrow purpose.[1] The factors that ensure that most people are law-abiding most of the time are not the impersonal threats of the law, but the disapproval of other individuals who know them and their own conscience which has been developed through such personal contact in the past.[2] Everyday life consists of government by men, not laws.[3] The law cannot make people good but other men and women can do so and much of the time they succeed in this. If benign influence is eroded by social change, then it is likely that there will be more crime.

Indeed, such a view is implicit in the work of the two classical builders of sociology, Emile Durkheim and Max Weber. Durkheim, writing at the turn of the century, saw modern society as increasingly characterized by *egoism*, a state in which individuals are but weakly attached to groups[4] and *anomie*, a state in which their lives are not regulated by moral norms and expectations and there are no limits to their appetites and ambitions.[5] He explored these trends in relation to urbanization and economic, religious and family life and although he investigated suicide rather than crime[6] as being both a result and an index of these social forces, later sociologists have used his work to explain the high rates of crime and deviance in the United States.[7] At about the same time Max Weber noted a trend in society towards the supremacy of large-scale, impersonal bureaucratic organizations, an effective tool for achieving material ends[8] but an iron cage[9] for the individuals caught up in them. Whereas at an earlier time people had worked at a calling because they saw it as the right thing to do, those employed in a large modern bureaucratic organization are merely constrained to comply with the rule book.[10] A large modern bureaucracy need not and does not concern itself with the overall character of its employees, ie whether they exhibit such qualities as diligence, reliability, probity, sobriety or self-control because those in charge believe they can obtain the required levels of productivity from them in more impersonal ways that seem to be cheaper.[11] Trust and standards are thus replaced by auditing and accountability. It is in fact a costly change but in the short-term much of the cost falls outside the organization and is of no interest to those running it. Once moral qualities cease to be important for employment and advancement, they are likely to be devalued and parents become far less concerned to ensure that their children acquire them.[12] A relational analysis thus does seem to provide an explanation for the marked rise, not just in crime, but also in illegitimacy and drug and alcohol abuse[13] during the last 40 years or so.

A long-term historical perspective
It would be quite wrong to suggest that long-term trends in crime can be explained in terms of a simple dichotomy between the small, supposedly crime-free communities of pre-industrial Britain and the criminogenic mass society of today. No such simple linear relationship exists. In particular there was a marked fall in the levels of recorded crime, both of crimes of violence and crimes of dishonesty, in the last half of the nineteenth century.[14] Since procedures for reporting and recording crime improved during this period, the real fall in levels of crime was probably even greater than that indicated by the statistics.[15] The incidence of illegitimacy also fell and, indeed, was lower in the cities than in remote rural areas.[16] There was also, towards the end of the period, a fall in drug and alcohol abuse.[17] Thus Britain in 1900 was a more crime-free and less deviant society than it is today *and* than it had been fifty years before and it is not possible to explain away this fact in terms of reporting and recording, nor of changes in the demographic structure of the population.

This creates a serious problem for the simple version of the relational theory of crime. Why should the incidence of crime fall in the late nineteenth century at a time when Britain was becoming a predominantly urban and industrial society, with people migrating in massive numbers away from the villages of the agricultural districts to seek work in industry or service occupations in large towns and cities? The factories, shops and offices in which people worked may have been smaller than those of today, but they were bigger than those that preceded them and the growth of a dense network of railways, and later of trams, in the course of the nineteenth century made mobility, and thus anonymity, easier and allowed people to live away from their work and commute. In the latter part of the nineteenth century the telephone and telegraph, the steamship and the mass-circulation newspaper likewise meant that ordinary people became aware of events in distant parts of the globe and even reacted to them as, say, in the case of Khartoum, Fashoda or Mafeking. The growth of limited liability, the stock market and investment banks separated ownership and control and greatly attenuated relationships between people at different points in the process of production. For workers, businessmen and professional people alike, it was a time of economic insecurity when a downturn could mean unemployment, bankruptcy, hardship and ruin. Distant impersonal economic forces could easily overwhelm personal economic relationships. In consequence, nineteenth century crime rates responded much more vigorously to the trade cycle than has been the case since the growth of state welfare provision.[18] During slumps the incidence of theft and other economic crimes rose, to fall in the boom that followed, while assaults and crimes of violence fell in a slump but rose again when employment and earnings picked up and more money was spent on alcohol.[19] Yet overall the *long-term* incidence of *both* kinds of crime *fell*.

It has been suggested that this is because overall standards of living rose in the late nineteenth century[20] and more and more of the working population had a reliable disposable income to spend on consumer goods for their families rather than periodic and unstable bonuses converted into extra alcohol.[21] Yet this also meant that there was more to steal and there is contemporary criticism of merchants in towns and cities who displayed their goods outside their stores in too tempting and accessible a fashion for potential thieves in the anonymous crowd passing their doors. If a simple version of relational theory is applied to this era, crime should have been rising and indeed many contemporary sociologists falsely believed that it was, because their theories predicted that it must be so.[22] But it was not rising; rates of crime certainly in Britain and probably in many other urbanizing and industrializing countries fell decisively in the latter half of the nineteenth century.[23]

The rise and decline of Relational institutions
The key problem facing the proponent of a relational analysis is that during the last century and a half there has been a steady movement in Britain away from small face-to-face communities and places of work characterized by personal contact, closeness and continuity towards large anonymous urban areas dominated by larger and larger, more and more impersonal, public and private corporations. However the pattern of crime and deviance follows a U-curve, falling in the late nineteenth century, reasonably stable in the first half of the twentieth and rising rapidly since the mid-1950s. A subtler relational explanation is needed, which can account for each phase by locating institutional changes that either directly or inversely follow the same pattern, ie a U-curve or an inverted

U-curve over the same periods of time, and which have important relational implications.

Church adherence

The first and most striking of these is the growth and decline in church adherence in England and Wales in relation to population, which rose in the late nineteenth century, peaked in about 1904-5; then an irregular decline with periods of recovery occurred until the late 1950s 'after which steep and thus far unremitting decline sets in'.[24] It is almost a mirror image of the trends in crime and deviance.

Table 1: Overall Trends During Three Periods of Time in England and Wales			
	1860-1905	1905-1960	1960 to present
Religious adherence and membership	Rising	Falling slowly and unevenly	Falling rapidly
Crimes of violence and dishonesty	Falling	Rising slowly and unevenly	Rising rapidly
Illegitimacy	Falling	Steady at a low level except in war-time	Rising rapidly
Drug and alcohol abuse	Falling unevenly	Falling to a low level	Rising

It may well be objected both that we do not know the *real* figures either for crime or for religious adherence and that in any case both church adherents and criminals were minorities in a largely honest but irreligious population. Neither objection disturbs the central argument which is that church adherence (in a positive sense) and criminality (in a negative sense) are indications of the strength of the values of respectability in British society. The churches were a key agency in promoting respectability in the nineteenth century and church adherence and attendance was one way in which respectability could be acquired, affirmed and expressed. Rising levels of adherence also gave those who were committed adherents the confidence to promote and foster the virtues of respectability among the majority of the population (who on the whole occupied a rather lower position in the social order than the adherents). These people were neither adherents nor attenders, but were receptive, albeit with reservations, to this religion-based social morality.

Sunday schools
In particular, non-adherents enrolled their children in Sunday schools not just to be rid of them for a few hours nor merely so that they would acquire useful secular skills associated with greater literacy, but in order that they might receive moral instruction. Over time, Sunday school enrolments in England and Wales show the same pattern of change as church adherence, but this involves a far larger proportion of the population. It has been estimated that 'between two-thirds and three quarters' of enrolled pupils 'generally attended on a Sunday'.[25]

Table 2: Sunday School Attendance[26]	
Year	% of population under 15 enrolled in Sunday school
1818	12
1851	38
1891	52
1901	53
1911	51
1931	46
1961	20
1989	14

Here again the pattern of rise and then fall is the mirror image of the pattern of fall and then rise to be found in the crime figures. In relational terms, it may be hypothesized that the Sunday schools were, at their peak, successful moral agents because they provided within an encounter relationship a form of moral instruction that was consistent with what parents and families sought for their children. The various significant adults in a child's life may have held quite different views about the more distant issues of politics or economics, but they constituted a common moral authority providing a consistent morality based on personal responsibility.

Friendly Societies

A similar pattern of rise followed by decline can be seen in another institution which provided a moral message through encounter relationships, namely the friendly societies which provided sickness benefits, medical care and support for widows and orphans. Also, to some extent, they provided unemployment and old age benefit for their members, most of whom had very modest earnings and little in the way of personal savings. The numbers enrolled in registered societies rose dramatically in the late nineteenth century from 2.7 million in 1877 to 3.6 million in 1887 to 4.8 million in 1897 and 6.6 million in 1910.[27] With the beginnings of the welfare state with Lloyd George's Insurance Act in 1911, the friendly societies became less important. With the development of a fully-fledged welfare state after World War II they entered a period of drastic decline.

The friendly societies were originally based on encounter relationships between individuals, who were able to trust one another and to co-operate in running a local society or branch of a society on a democratic basis and whose sense of fraternity and solidarity was reinforced by shared rituals and celebrations.[28] Members were less likely to try to cheat a society based on personal contact and mutuality than a distant organization such as an insurance company or the state which might well be seen in adversarial terms. Also the members could and did police their own colleagues' actions not just in regard to claims for benefit, or to restrain imprudent or immoral behaviour that might damage the society financially or give it a bad name, but as part of what they saw as a valid aspect of a character-building association.[29]

In the course of the twentieth century the friendly societies have been largely superseded by state welfare or by large commercial insurance companies and pension funds. These are more efficient as a way of pooling major risks but being impersonal bureaucracies based on contingent relationships, they lack the moral dimension of their predecessors. Indeed, the beginnings of this trend may be seen at the peak of importance of the the friendly societies, for some individual friendly societies who, as they grew in size and established large numbers of branches, became more bureaucratic and impersonal in their mode of operation.[30] Nonetheless, the rise of such institutions and their subsequent replacement by a bureaucratic welfare state may, as Stephen Davies[31] has pointed out, have contributed to the moralization and subsequent demoralization of British society. It has also been argued that if welfare provision were made on a local encounter-relationship and judgmental basis, as in Switzerland, it would produce a lower incidence of crime.[32]

The moral code of personal responsibility broke down in Britain in the twentieth century as people came to see the anonymity of urban living and of bureaucratic institutions as their normal way of life rather than something to be fought against in an attempt to re-create and indeed improve upon the remembered small communities of their own past. The churches and Sunday schools flourished most when the larger towns were growing in size due to migration from outside rather than from their own natural population increase. Once a town came to consist almost entirely of second or third generation urbanites, the churches and Sunday schools seem to have lost their hold on the people living there.[33] Only the transplanted seem to need a heart in a heartless world.

Moral change and the world of work

A similar sequence of moralization followed by subsequent demoralization during three successive phases of industrial development in Britain has been pointed out with great insight by Bryan R Wilson. In the first phase of his model, when most people still lived in small rural communities, morality at work and in other aspects of life was made effective mainly through immediate social controls, ie through the feelings of the other members of face-to-face groups constituted by neighbours, kin and community. However in Wilson's second phase, with the growth of an urban industrial economy in Britain, the new work order demanded a new kind and degree of morality in which diffuse social controls were supplemented by a more intense socialization of the individual.

> Work was being moralized. It had become a separated and well defined sphere of activity, no longer embedded for the mass of men in home, kinship and local community . . . good work depended on willingness, sobriety, trust and commitment and the moral undertaking to give of one's best.'[34]

In this new moral universe the value of personal responsibility—though already present in the old face-to-face world—came to be stressed even more strongly because of the higher degree of self-regulation and self-control demanded of the individual workers in the new industries of the nineteenth century. It was necessary that they be diligent, honest and reliable even in the absence of surveillance by others. At that time

> . . . the best guarantee of a man's being a good worker [was]the assurance that he [was] also a good man. It became quite common in late nineteenth century

Britain, for any worker of the humbler sort to rely, not merely and perhaps not mainly, on any certification of his technical skills . . . but on evidence of his moral worth. He often had, sometimes literally in an envelope in his breast pocket, what he called 'my character'—a testimonial that he was the possessor of those prized moral virtues: honesty, willingness, industry, conscientiousness, a sense of responsibility, punctuality and sobriety.'[35]

Finally, speaking of our own time Bryan Wilson notes that

. . . the third phase of my model is that of the demoralization both of work and of the wider reaches of the social order . . . the new work order gradually ceased to be dependent on the general morality inculcated in early industrialization . . . once conveyor belts, electronic controls, automation and computers came into wider use, it became less necessary to depend for performance on the moral commitment of the worker . . . the modern worker does not need to have been socialized for a predominantly moral role . . . The economy can get from its workers the performance it requires without imposing on parents the burden and rigours that were attendant on the long, slow and intensive personal socialization process of the past.[36]

The great strength of Bryan Wilson's clear and convincing argument is that he takes account of and seeks to explain each stage of the U-curve in the moralization and demoralization of British society. However, it is difficult to see why the organization of work should *necessarily* be the independent variable producing and causing moral change. It may well be that the drive to monitor a person's work in impersonal ways (which are often ineffective) is rather the *result* of a decline in the strength of individual moral character, much as shops now monitor their customers through television cameras because of the increased incidence of shop-lifting. Theft produces surveillance, not the other way round.

From moralism to causalism
The steady, continued and possibly accelerating rise of bureaucracy in the twentieth century has not only meant that relationships between individuals have become more contingent but has also caused the moral thinking of an increasingly bureaucratic elite to move away from a concern with personal moral responsibility and to adopt a 'causalist' ethic. Causalism is a form of short-run negative utilitarianism that aims to regulate individuals and their relationships so as to minimise harm and suffering overall, regardless of the moral status or past behaviour of the individuals involved.[37] The causalist mode of tackling moral questions developed originally because it was the most appropriate way of regulating interactions between large bureaucratic organizations. Business corporations, government departments and trade unions are not individuals and the interactions between them tend to be increasingly seen as issues of cause and effect, accountability and liability rather than praise and

blame, reward and punishment.[38] Rules of strict liability or 'knock for knock' agreements between insurance companies are likewise ways of bypassing questions of deserts or blame in the interests of reducing harm overall or of avoiding expensive disputes and producing predictable albeit sometimes unfair outcomes. In each of these impersonal modes of procedure the relational element is largely absent or has been excluded; likewise causalism is an ethic largely devoid of relational considerations.

As early as the end of the nineteenth century, when moralist ideals of personal responsibility had spread throughout the social order such that the incidence of crime and much other deviant behaviour was at its minimum, the alternative causalist morality outlined above began to take root among the officials concerned with formulating and implementing social policy. Martin Wiener has noted that:

> Even as the image of autonomous and effective, but self-restraining, Protestant man established in the first half of the century was strengthening its hold on social classes beneath them, members of the official classes were finding that image increasingly unconvincing intellectually and unsatisfying emotionally . . . As both the practicality and the humanity of insisting upon an individual's responsibility for his fate came into question the once-dominant policy outlook of moralism—the distribution of benefits and penalties according to the moral deserts of the people involved in a situation—was losing its consensual force. In its place was emerging a new outlook . . . causalism.[39]

During the twentieth century the causalist outlook grew in strength in Britain and by the 1960s it was the dominant moral outlook in Parliament and the basis of the law reforms of that decade involving abortion, divorce, homosexuality and capital punishment.[40] In and of itself it seems to be a reasonable and respectable moral outlook for those engaged in the provision of welfare or of reforming the law, but it is derived from the problems involved in regulating large, anonymous institutions[41] and is likely to undermine as well as ignore what Schluter and Lee have termed the relational factor (or 'R-Factor').[42]

Whereas in Britain in the last half of the nineteenth century people responded to urban anonymity and uncertainty by the spontaneous creation of institutions that provided new personal relationships and a stronger personal moral ethic, in the twentieth century all British institutions and moral thinking have become permeated with an impersonal ethos. The fall and subsequent rise in such social problems as crime, illegitimacy and drug and drink abuse is thus a product of the rise and subsequent fall of the R-Factor during the development of an urban and industrial society in Britain.

Conclusion

The most important conclusions to be derived from an historical analysis of crime in relation to the rise and fall of the relational order in British society are of necessity general, rather than amounting to specific policy proposals. The first point to note is that there is not a rigid unilinear relationship between urbanization and industrialisation and the shift from encounter relationships to contingent ones. The experiences both of Victorian England and probably also of modern Japan and other East Asian societies seem to show that encounter relationships can and do survive this kind of social change. The second point is that in Victorian Britain at least encounter relationships were deliberately fostered by the voluntary and spontaneous action of the people who created relational institutions in a *gesellschaft* society; they were not creations of the state. Indeed it may well be that it is difficult for the state to pursue pro-relational policies, because, almost by definition, the institutions of state that would have to be used for this purpose are impersonal bureaucracies that can only deal with purely contingent relationships.

Notes

1 M Schluter, and D Lee, *The R-Factor* (London: Hodder and Stoughton, 1993).
2 J Burnside, *Relational Justice # 1 The Relational Causes of Crime* (Cambridge: Jubilee Policy Group, 1993), pp 6-7.
3 The alternative is government by lawyers.
4 See E Durkheim, 1952 (1897) *Suicide* (London: Routledge Kegan Paul, 1952 [1987]), pp 367-9, 373-4.
5 E Durkheim, 1952 (1897) pp 246-54, 358.
6 E Durkheim, *The Rules of Sociological Method* (New York: Free Press, 1938 [1895])p 75.
7 For example R K Merton, 'Social Structure and Anomie' in *Social Theory and Social Structure* (Glencoe: Free Press, 1957).
8 M Weber, in H Gerth and C W Mills (trans and eds) *From Max Weber: Essays in Sociology* (London: Routledge and Kegan Paul, 1948), notably pp 228-9.
9 M Weber, *The Protestant Ethic and the Spirit of Capitalism* (London: Unwin, 1930 [1920]) p 181.
10 *Ibid.* p 181.
11 B R Wilson, 'Morality in the Evolution of the Social System', *British Journal of Sociology*, vol 3 (1985), pp 315-32.
12 *Ibid* p 321.
13 L Radzinowicz, and J King, *The Growth of Crime* (Harmondsworth: Penguin, 1979) and for subsequent years *Criminal Statistics England and Wales* (London: HMSO). C Davies, *Permissive Britain, Social Change in the Sixties and Seventies* (London: Pitman, 1975), pp 67,140-2, 156-6.
14 V A C Gatrell, and T B Hadden, 'Criminal Statistics and their Interpretation' in E A Wrigley ed, *Nineteenth Century: Essays in the use of Quantitative Methods for the Study of Social Data* (Cambridge: Cambridge U P 1972). V A C Gatrell, 'The Decline of Theft in Victorian and Edwardian England' in V A C Gatrell ed, *Crime and the Law: the Social History of Crime in Western Europe since 1500* (London: Europa, 1980).

15 Gatrell, and Hadden (1972), p 374; W L Melville Lee, *A History of Police in England* (London: Methuen, 1901).

16 S Foster Hartley, *Illegitimacy* (Berkeley: University of California Press, 1975); P Laslett, *Family Life and Illicit Love in Earlier Generations* (Cambridge: Cambridge U P, 1977), pp 113, 119, 123, 157.

17 See G B Wilson, *Alcohol and the Nation* (London: Nicholson and Watson, 1940); and A E Dingle, 'Drink and Working Class Living Standards in Britain 1870-1914' in D Oddy and D Miller, eds, *The Making of the Modern British Diet* (London: Croom Helm, 1975).

18 See Gatrell, and Hadden (1972), V A C Gattrell (1980) and J Sarnecki, 'Some Mechanisms of the Growth of Crime in Sweden', *Archiwum Kryminologii*, T XII (1985), pp 199-210.

19 Sarnecki (1985), L O Pike, *A History of Crime in England* II (London: Smith Elder, 1876), p 584.

20 Gatrell, and Hadden (1972), p 377.

21 See Dingle (1975).

22 L Macdonald, 'Theory and Evidence of Rising Crime in the Nineteenth Century', *British Journal of Sociology*, Vol 33 No 3 (1982), pp 4-20.

23 For Britain see Gattrell and Hadden (1972), Gattrell (1980). For Sweden see Sarnecki, (1985).

24 C G Brown, 'A Revisionist Approach to Religious Change' in S Bruce ed, *Religion and Modernization* (Oxford: Clarendon, 1992), (pp 31-58), p 45. See also pp 42-4.

25 R Gill in S Bruce, ed, *Religion and Modernization* (Oxford: Clarendon, 1992), pp 90-117, p 96.

26 From R. Gill, pp 96-7. See also T W Laqueur, *Religion and Respectability; Sunday Schools and Working Class Culture 1780-1850* (New Haven: Yale U P) p 246; D Martin, *A Sociology of English Religion* (London: Heinemann, 1967), pp 41-2; A Wilkinson, *The Church of England and the First World War* (London: SPCK, 1978), p 7.

27 D G Green, *Reinventing Civil Society* (London: IEA Health and Welfare Unit, 1993), Choice in Welfare Series No 7, pp 31-2. See also P H J H Gosden, *The Friendly Societies in England 1815-75* (Manchester: Manchester U P, 1960), pp 212-3 and P H J H Godsen, *Self-Help, Voluntary Association in the 19th Century* (London: Batsford, 1973), pp 91, 103-4.

28 See Gosden (1960), pp 115-37.

29 Green (1993), pp 46-53, 56-7.

30 Gosden (1960), pp 214-20.

31 S Davies, 'Towards the Remoralization of Society' in M Loney *et al* eds, *The State or the Market* (London: Sage, 1987), pp 172-88.

32 M Clinard, *Cities with Little Crime; the Case of Switzerland* (Cambridge: Cambridge U P, 1978), C Davies, 'Crime, Bureaucracy and Equality', *Policy Review*, 23 (1983), pp 89-105, R Segalman, *The Swiss Way of Welfare, Lessons for the Western World* (Buffalo: Praeger, 1986).

33 J Manson, *The Nonconformists* (London: SPCK, 1991), pp 301-4.

34 Wilson (1985), p 320.

35 *Ibid.* p 319.

36 *Ibid.* p 320-21.

37 C Davies, (1975), pp 5-7, C Davies, 'Moralists Causalists, Sex, Law and Morality' in W H G Armytage, R Chester, and J Peel, eds, *Changing Patterns of Sexual Behaviour* (London: Academic, 1980).

38 *Ibid.* pp 207-10.

39 M Wiener, *Reconstructing the Criminal, Culture Law and Policy in England 1830-1914* (Cambridge: Cambridge U P, 1990), pp 357-8.

40 C Davies (1975), pp 13-44 and 1980.

41 *Ibid.* pp 207-10.

42 M Schluter and D Lee (1993)

CHAPTER 3

Tension and Tradition in the Pursuit of Justice

Jonathan Burnside

We have an intuitive awareness of what justice is which seems to lie at the core of our being. In the legends of ancient Greece, it is the imparting by Hermes of 'a sense of justice' that differentiates man from the beasts. The purpose of this chapter is to offer some reflection on the meaning of justice. This is central not only to a proper discussion of the values and goals of the criminal justice system but perhaps also to what it means to be human. 'To be human is to know justice'.[1]

Of course, knowing justice in an intuitive sense and articulating what it means are two different things. Justice is a term which is debated over and over again in the history of ideas and yet remains the subject of chronic dispute. It is an 'essentially contested concept'. The first major work on the subject, *The Republic*, aptly takes the form of a series of dialogues. But whilst Plato's conversants, and their many successors, have come and gone the dialogue continues. The debate on justice is never foreclosed.

One of the questions which Relational Justice raises is whether it is legitimate to juxtapose 'relationships', in the sense of human dynamics generally, with 'justice'. Naturally, it depends on how one conceptualises justice. At one extreme, where justice is seen as the mechanical application of rules, the juxtaposition of 'relationships' with 'justice' seems a contradiction in terms. How are human dynamics to be reconciled with the logic of legalism? At the other extreme, the juxtaposition collapses into tautology. If justice, in its supra-legal sense, is about the ordering of society and how things should relate to each other, how can this not involve relationships? So on the one hand, the words 'Relational' and 'Justice' seem to repel each other, while on the other hand, they appear to be synonymous. The problem is resolved by recognising that there is an inherent tension within Relational Justice which prevents it from becoming simply one or the other.

Justice in its intuitive sense is not completely repelled by the relational dimension because the one coheres with the other in a way that two words that were randomly chosen would not. But they are not synonymous. The relational component highlights the importance of human relationships to understanding and doing justice and thus it avoids tautology. They cohere, but they are distinctive. Because they simultaneously attract and repel each other, a tension lies at the heart of Relational Justice.

The purpose of this chapter is to explore this tension by reference to three pairs of issues that draw on current debates in the fields of law, psychology and political philosophy. The issues are respectively: antiseptic and passionate construals of justice; gender perceptions of morality; and the problems faced by philosophers in talking about justice in a post-Enlightenment, plural society. Each represents a tension of its own. Together, they aim to provide a theoretical overview of Relational Justice and a justification for the relational processes that are advocated elsewhere in this volume, such as the New Zealand youth justice system. Hence it is to these that the reader should turn in seeking the following ideas in tangible form.

Antiseptic and passionate construals

Construals arise from the common distinction that can be drawn between things of first and second order, that is, between what a thing is in and of itself (the first order) and the different ways in which it can be talked about (the second order). A construal is therefore a second order activity because it is a way of seeing or interpreting something that belongs to the first order.

Justice is something that belongs to the first order whose existence we intuit. But there are many different ways in which we can talk about justice because it is a word which, due to its long and dense past, has come to concentrate within itself a range of meanings and definitions.

An antiseptic construal of justice would emphasise objectivity, impartiality and the fair application of rules, whilst a passionate construal of justice would emphasise love, compassion and the vindication of the weak. Both are integral to our understanding of justice. But problems arise when one eclipses the other.

How does modern culture encourage us to construe criminal justice? Iconographically, criminal justice is equated with the statue of Justicia, standing blindfold atop the Old Bailey with the scales of justice in one hand and a sword in the other. The blindfold, the scales and the sword symbolise impartiality, the thoroughness of a fair trial and the sureness of punishment.

Justicia is an icon that captures much, but also misses much. She celebrates the antiseptic construals of objectivity, neutrality and fairness and sterilises the passionate construals that equally make the intuitive knowledge of what is just part of what it means to be human.

Modern culture encourages us to adopt an antiseptic construal of justice, at both theoretical and practical levels. At a theoretical level it is apparent in the proposition that it is impossible for a judge ever to show mercy.[2] A state, so the argument runs, must always act rationally if it is to remain accountable. But mercy is irrational because it involves suspending the normal rules of justice so that some people are specially treated. Since something that is purely rational cannot also be merciful, it follows there are no circumstances in which the state can be justified in showing mercy. Only by forgoing mercy can we enable the state to behave like a fully rational entity, accountable for all its actions to the people over whom it has power.

At a practical level, the antiseptic side of justice is seen in the desire for uniform rather than individualised responses to crime and criminals. Taking their lead from the baseball slogan 'three strikes, you're out', legislators in the USA propose that an offender should be automatically jailed on a third indictable offence. A similar form of mandatory sentence that has been put forward in this country is a '3-3-3' system whereby mandatory custodial sentences of 3 days, 3 months and 3 years would be imposed for first, second and third arrestable offences respectively. The only exceptions to this 'jail-for-all' formula would be relatively minor crimes such as shoplifting. Part and parcel of this antiseptic construal is the tendency to see justice in terms of technology in which computer-aided judgments and sentencing grids are deployed to ensure 'consistency'.

The shortcoming of the antiseptic approach is that it leads to an undue preoccupation with the process of justice to the detriment of the final outcome that those processes are meant to secure.

Consequently, an antiseptic construal needs to be complemented by a passionate construal of justice which highlights the need for love, compassion, outrage and mercy. So dominant is the antiseptic construal in modern thought that justice and love, for example, are usually treated as polar opposites. But in fact, both justice and love converge on what is essential for individual harmony and social well-being, that is, right relationships. As Philip Allott writes, if 'justice is the mathematics of society',[3] 'love is, perhaps, the mathematics of being human'.[4]

At a practical level, the passionate side of justice is seen in taking proper cognisance of the individual features of the case and responding accordingly. The recent recommendation to abolish the mandatory life sentence for murder is a good example.[5] Since the classes of offence covered by the common law definition vary widely in character and culpability— including so-called 'mercy-killings', battered wives who kill under provocation, as well as premeditated homicides—it is argued that discretionary penalties are needed to allow a flexible response. The fact that this recommendation has been rejected possibly indicates how deeply ingrained the antiseptic construal remains. Another recent example of a passionate construal is Lord Justice Lawton's recognition that a lobster stolen from a fisherman's pot in Cornwall may be a qualitatively different crime than the theft of a lobster from the deep-freeze in Harrods. Judges daily use their discretion to give an individualised response to the human dynamics that lie behind the crime.

In this way Justicia, on her own, is an inadequate idol for the criminal justice system. Justice is about more than due process. Above all, it reflects our desire to live in right relationship. Like chimpanzees and termites, we are social beings and this in turn requires that we be law-abiding. Thus the ancient Greeks record that the purpose of justice is 'to bring order into our cities and create a bond of friendship of union'.[6] Justice draws society towards the ideal of right relationships between people and things, giving it 'a pole of attraction'.[7] The entire legal process, including (perhaps especially) the criminal justice system ought to be a continually-changing actualisation of this seeking of society.

Thus the first strand of Relational Justice argues that there is a need to maintain a dialectic between antiseptic and passionate construals of justice. Just as in music counterpoint is produced when two or more independent parts are combined in a harmonious texture so the goal of Relational Justice, as a 'second order' construct, is to produce counterpoint between two independent, yet indispensable, construals of justice.

Gender perceptions of morality and justice

The tension noted between the passionate and the antiseptic virtues finds a parallel with the next pair of issues, namely, gender perceptions of morality and justice. This constitutes the second strand of what makes justice relational.

This strand is teased out of developmental psychology, specifically, moral development. The contrast here is between a 'masculine' view of justice which can be seen in retrospect in the work of Lawrence Kohlberg and a 'feminine' view which has been highlighted by the work of Carol Gilligan.[8] The tension is between a masculine perception of justice which is based on a 'rights' approach to morality and a feminine perception that is based on conflicting responsibilities rather than competing rights. The contrast is between a masculine mode of thinking which is formal and abstract and a feminine approach which is contextual and narrative.

'Rights' stress separation and emphasise the individual as primary; wheras 'responsibility' stresses interdependence and emphasises relationships. And whilst the masculine conception ties moral development to an understanding of rights and rules, the feminine conception centres moral development around the understanding of responsibility and relationships.

Empirical support for this divergence is found in Gilligan's own research which used samples of school children of both sexes, female college students and women who had undergone abortion. From her sample of school children, the contrasting responses of two eleven-year-olds, a boy and a girl, to a typical 'moral dilemma' provides an illustration.

The moral dilemma which drew out the children's perceptions of what was just invited them to consider whether a man named Heinz should steal a drug that he cannot afford to buy in order to save his wife's life. From the same moral dilemma two very different moral problems emerged.

The boy saw the dilemma, in his words, as 'sort of like a math problem with humans', which could be solved impersonally through systems of logic and law. He saw a straight conflict between life and property and, casting it as an impersonal conflict of claims, looked to the law to mediate the dispute. He abstracted the moral problem from the interpersonal situation, and found in the logic of fairness an objective way to decide who should win.

The girl, on the other hand, saw the problem in relationship-oriented terms. The internal structure of the problem arose not from the chemist's assertion of rights but from his failure to respond to Heinz' wife. Because the girl saw, in Gilligan's terms, 'a world that coheres through human connection rather than through systems of rules'[9], the solution is found in the confident belief that '[if Heinz and the chemist] had talked it out long enough they could reach something besides stealing'.[10] As members of a network of relationships on whose existence they all depend, her solution is mediated, not impersonally through logic or law, but 'personally through communication in relationship'.[11]

Both solutions are the product of rational processes, but they diverge because they arise from different understandings of morality and justice. The boy set up a hierarchical ordering to resolve conflict; the girl described a network of relationships; the former responded categorically, the latter contextually, and so on.

Together they offer a complementary and more comprehensive image of justice and conflict resolution. A vision of justice which sought only to give expression to one or other would be inadequate. It would be 'like the sound of one hand clapping.'[12]

The first pair of issues identified a tension between the 'antiseptic' and the 'passionate' construals of justice which parallels the tension between masculine and feminine perceptions of what is just. Just as resolution of the former was sought in 'counterpoint' so the goal, again, is not complete integration ('Hermaphrodite' justice) but rather an ongoing dialectic in which each learns from and respects the other. And just as the first pair of issues anticipated the second, so the second pair of issues anticipates the third, namely the contrast between liberal and tradition-based approaches to justice.

Post-Enlightenment justice: liberalism versus tradition

The one-sided emphasis upon 'impartiality' and 'fairness' that is found in the image of Justicia and the tendency Gilligan found among men to resolve moral problems abstractly with reference to 'rights' and reason finds a resounding echo in modern liberal theories of justice, and indeed in the foundations of liberalism itself.

(i) The liberal approach

Liberalism emerged from a number of beliefs that came into their own during the eighteenth century. These included the freedom of the individual from arbitrary external authority, the individual as the source of his or her own moral values, the regulation of social life by universal and impersonal laws and equal opportunity for all. For better, or for worse, it is the political philosophy that has shaped the Western world over the past several hundred years.[13]

Few would slight its positive impact. Liberalism established decisively the equality of all people—together with the civil rights that implied—and it produced the basic concepts of much that is admirable in Western forms of government, such as the rights of the individual and democracy.

Yet it is a commonplace criticism that liberalism centres on the individual at the expense of those relationships which alone can nurture human well-being. Liberalism, it is alleged, promotes the view that people do not need other people: 'all they need is a system of rules that will constitute procedures for resolving disputes as they pursue their various interests.'[14] Of course, many liberals would reject such a charge as a caricature, but it is fair to detect in liberal visions of justice a strong bias towards individualist values.

Many different approaches can be taken to the question of justice within liberal legal theory. But broadly speaking, there are two main types of approach which Margaret Moore calls 'justice as mutual advantage' and 'justice as impartiality'.[15]

Justice as mutual advantage regards justice as a compromise between man's selfish nature and the need for an orderly society. But it is only a compromise and has no other authority: justice is simply the price we pay for forgoing our natural instincts. Since its animating idea is that the principles of justice have to be acceptable to each person subject to them, Thomas Hobbes' *Leviathan*, which first expressed the idea of a 'social contract', is seen as a good example.

Justice as impartiality holds that the principles of justice should be acceptable to each person when that person is stripped of his or her individuality. This type of approach can also be modelled on 'contractual' terms. John Rawls' *A Theory of Justice*[16] is a contemporary exposition.

He pictures a group of rational individuals who have to agree on a set of principles that will govern the basic structure of their society. They are to choose these principles on the grounds of rational self-interest, but their choice is constrained by the fact that they are deprived of certain types of knowledge about themselves. They are to choose, as Rawls puts it, from behind a 'veil of ignorance'. The veil of ignorance excludes knowledge of all those features that make one person different from another. Thus the people in 'the original position', as Rawls calls the basic choice situation, do not know what gender they are, what abilities they have or to which social class they belong. In this state they unanimously decide upon principles of justice. These will be impartial, 'not only in the sense that they apply impartially, but also in the sense that they are chosen from the standpoint of the original position, which is an interpretation of impartiality itself'.[17]

To critics, the weakness of both liberal approaches is that they tend to emphasise the autonomy of the individual at the expense of the communal relationships in which they are embedded. Not surprisingly, Rawls' theory, with its emphasis upon abstract selves making autonomous choices has been described as 'the best-known articulation of justice for modern liberalism'.[18] It is a highly artificial scenario. Ironically, Rawls' attempt to construct a neutral theory of justice is itself a violation of neutrality. For example, Rawls' first 'impartial' principle of justice arbitrarily assumes that the 'political' liberties (such as freedom of speech) are important constituents of a worthwhile life whereas the 'market' liberties (such as freedom of property) are not. Rawls also adjusts the veil of ignorance to ensure that the principles which are chosen are the principles that he wishes to argue for. But even the very idea that there is some neutral vantage-point from which one can talk about justice is open to challenge.

For one critic, Stanley Hauerwas, Rawls' theory stands as a testimony to 'the moral limits of the liberal tradition'.[19] The original position is 'a stark metaphor for the ahistorical approach of liberal theory, as the self is alienated from its history and simply left with its individual preferences and prejudices'.[20] Liberalism, on his view, is successful because 'it supplies us with a myth that seems to make sense of our social origins'.[21] The myth is that a people do not need a shared history; all they need is a 'system of rules' or a 'social contract'. But a system of rules is not enough. The social and political validity of a community results from its being formed by a story: that process of historical bonding and sense of continuity which provides a framework for living. Relationships are central to this process, shaping and sustaining the narrative of human development through communication.

That we are free to make up our own stories—that the individual is the sole source of authority—is consistent with the humanism of the Enlightenment, to which modern liberalism owes a considerable debt. The Enlightenment generated intense hostility to the past in the belief that reason would ultimately displace authority and tradition as a source of truth. However, this enormous faith in the powers of reason was shown to be misplaced when the Enlightenment thinkers and their successors could not be found to agree on what these principles were that could be affirmed by all rational persons. As a result, the legacy of the Enlightenment has been the 'ultimacy of disagreement'. After all, how can we come to agreed conclusions in our culture when we lack not only a shared set of moral values but also standards of rational justification by which to determine right from wrong? According to Alasdair MacIntyre, the way out of the debris caused by the collapse of the Enlightenment ideal is, surely, to ask what alternative mode of understanding the Enlightenment rejected. What was it that failed to fit into its vision of the world? His answer to 'what the Enlightenment made us for the most part blind to, and what we now need to recover is . . . a conception of rational enquiry as embodied in a tradition'[22] : what he terms a 'tradition of enquiry'.

(ii) Traditions of enquiry
A tradition is an argument extended through time, from which standards of rational justification emerge as part of a history. Different traditions embody different visions of what is just and since there are a diversity of traditions of enquiry, there are multiple contending accounts of justice.

This approach gives the lie to the liberal assumption that it is possible to assess and justify a particular moral tradition from some neutral vantage-point. Rather, it is only from within traditions that anyone is able to acquire the standing-ground or the vocabulary from which to reject or defend particular ethical practices. The one who stands outside all traditions is a mute.

In *Whose Justice? Which Rationality?* MacIntyre presents an outline history of three traditions of enquiry into what rationality is and what justice is. The details do not concern us here; suffice it to say that the traditions are in antagonistic relationship, having very different histories and contending accounts of justice. His conclusion is that 'there is no other way to engage in the formulation, elaboration, rational justification, and criticism of accounts of . . . justice . . . apart from that which is provided by some particular tradition or other.'[23]

It is an approach which faces squarely the problem of diversity of opinion. To this extent it accepts some measure of plurality. But pluralism and relativism are rejected because mutually antagonistic beliefs or contending accounts of justice cannot be equally true. Just as a scientific theory survives its claim to be true by the existence of supporting data, so a tradition of enquiry survives if it can overcome the dissolution of well-founded certitudes. Traditions defeat and are defeated by other traditions depending on how well they are able to overcome 'epistemological crises'.[24]

Hence, just as there was a contrast between the antiseptic and the passionate construals of justice which anticipated the contrast between masculine and feminine perceptions, so both pairs anticipate and link up with the third pair of contrasts, that between liberal and tradition-based approaches to understanding justice. Whereas the liberal approach would tend to emphasise the autonomy of the individual, impartiality and abstraction, a tradition-based approach looks to narrative, history and community to understand the meaning of justice.

The first two strands of Relational Justice argue for an ongoing dialectic between antiseptic and passionate construals of justice and between male and female perceptions of justice and conflict resolution. The third strand rejects reason alone as a sufficient basis for understanding justice and argues that the meaning of justice, in a post-Enlightenment, plural society should take place within the context of a particular tradition of enquiry.

This raises the obvious question: is there a tradition of enquiry to which Relational Justice is particularly indebted and/or within which it may develop? We can only answer this question if we recognise that behind each tradition of enquiry is a still more basic worldview. Dr Harold Turner observes that strictly

> . . . there are only three possible ways of understanding the world: the atomic, the oceanic, and the relational—symbolised respectively by billiard balls, the ocean, and the net . . . The atomic, which is characteristic of contemporary Western society and has deep roots in Greek philosophy, sees reality in terms of its individual units. The atom, conceived as a minute piece of matter, is the ultimate constituent of the visible world. The human individual, conceived as an autonomous center of knowing and willing, is the ultimate constituent of society. The oceanic view, on the other hand, sees all things ultimately merged into one entity which is both the soul and all that exists . . . The third view sees everything as constituted by relationships, whether it is the material world or human society.[25]

Relational Justice is inspired by a relational view of the person. Indeed, the term 'person', properly understood, has a significance which the word 'individual' lacks. The word 'individual' emphasises the separateness of the person, whereas 'person' underscores the fact that we are constituted by relationships; that is, our identity, even our being, is dependent upon the fact of relationship. We do not simply need relationships to be fulfilled; we need relationships *to be*. 'To be is to be in relationship'.[26]

In the history of Western thought the possibility of conceiving humanity in fundamentally relational terms is traced by many scholars to the arrival of Christianity and its consequent impact upon philosophy. Colin Gunton argues that 'there exist in the Western tradition two distinct though sometimes overlapping views of the person, one of them believed almost everywhere, but wrong; the other neglected, but right'. [27]

The mainstream view is expressed in Descartes' idea that the person is the mind, which produces an individualist view of the human person. The alternative view is represented by John Macmurray: '. . . the self exists only in dynamic relation with the other'.[28] Thus 'I need "you" in order to be "myself"'.[29] As Gunton himself puts it, *'As persons we are only what we are, in relation to other persons . . . '* (his italics).[30] Possible antecedents, within Western thought, to this relational view of the person are the work of Sir William Hamilton, a nineteenth century Scottish philosopher who was directly or indirectly influenced by Calvin, and the doctrine of the Trinity developed by Richard of St Victor in the twelfth century.

In this way, we owe an intellectual debt to Jewish and Christian teaching for a relational understanding of the person. And there remains, in the modern context, a degree of compatibility between a Relational perspective and one favoured by Jewish and Christian teaching.

Thus, if it is the case that a relational understanding of reality is close to the Biblical worldview, then some of the convictions associated with Jewish and Christian beliefs may find a parallel with Relational Justice.

Conclusion

Tensions and traditions are integral to the pursuit of justice. A dialectic needs to be maintained between antiseptic and passionate construals of justice as well as between masculine and feminine perceptions, if there is to be any prospect that just procedures will result in just outcomes. Furthermore, the lesson to be learnt from the collapse of the Enlightenment ideal is that reason alone will not give us an adequate grasp of the meaning of justice. Rather, justice needs to be pursued within a community of people who are prepared to agree upon certain aims and assumptions of which the most essential that has been identified in this chapter is the conception of human beings as essentially relational.

Traditions of enquiry which derive from a relational worldview draw on the heritage which Jewish and Christian teaching has bequeathed to Western thought and propel us towards the ideal of justice. It is an ideal that can only be realised in the context of relationships, for above all, justice is a community responsibility, with community obligations.

Notes

1 Plato,*The Republic* (tr Desmond Lee, London: Penguin, 1987).

2 R Harrison, 'The equality of mercy', in R. Harrison and H. Gross, eds, *Jurisprudence: Cambridge Essays* (Oxford: Oxford University Press, 1992)

3 P Allott, *Eunomia: A New Order for a New World* (Oxford: Oxford University Press, 1990), p 82.

4 *Ibid.* p 84.

5 Prison Reform Trust *Report of the Committee on the Penalty for Homicide* (London: Prison Reform Trust, 1994).

6 Plato, 'Protagaras', in E Hamilton and H Cairns, eds, *The Collected Dialogues of Plato* Bollingen Series (XXI), (Princeton: Princeton University Press).

7 Allott, *op.cit.* p 83.

8 For both see C Gilligan, *In a Different Voice* (Mass: Harvard University Press, 1993).

9 *Ibid*, p 29.

10 *Ibid.* p 29.

11 *Ibid*, p 29.

12 *Ibid.* p 160.

13 See generally H J Laski, *The Rise of European Liberalism* (London: Unwin Books, 1962).

14 S Hauerwas, *A Community of Character* (London: University of Notre Dame Press, 1981), p 78.

15 M Moore, *Foundations of Liberalism* (Oxford: Clarendon Press, 1993), p 9ff.

16 J Rawls, *A Theory of Justice* (Oxford: Oxford University Press, 1972)

17 Moore, *op cit.*, p 35.

18 S C Mott, *A Christian Perspective on Political Thought* (New York: Oxford University Press, 1993), p 142.

19 Hauerwas, *op cit.*, p 82.

20 *Ibid*, p 78.

21 *Ibid.*, p 82.

22 A MacIntyre, *Whose Justice? Which Rationality?* (London: Duckworth, 1988), p 7.

23 *Ibid.*, p 350.

24 *Ibid.*, p 362.

25 Cited in L Newbigin, *The Gospel in a Pluralist Society* (London: SPCK, 1989), pp 171-2.

26 M Schluter and D Lee, *The R-Factor* (London: Hodder and Stoughton, 1993).

27 C E Gunton, *The Promise of Trinitarian Theology* (Edinburgh: T&T Clark, 1975), p 86.

28 J Macmurray, *Persons in Relation* (London: Faber and Faber, 1961), p 17.

29 *Ibid.* p 69.

30 Gunton, *op. cit*, pp 90-1.

CHAPTER 4

Avoiding Injustice, Promoting Legitimacy and Relationships

Anthony Bottoms

The concept of 'Relational Justice', proposed by the Jubilee Policy Group as of relevance to debates in criminal justice (Schluter and Lee 1993, ch 9) has, for me, considerable appeal. My understanding of the concept, however, perhaps differs somewhat from that of the Jubilee Group, and the main purpose of this chapter is to explain the approach that I would adopt to the relevant theoretical issues[1]. The content of this chapter is, quite unashamedly, theoretical; but it is not intended to be either inaccessible or irrelevant to practitioners in the various criminal justice services. Rather, what I hope to suggest is that the concept of 'relational justice'—or, as I would now prefer to phrase the matter, the goal of 'avoiding injustice and promoting legitimacy and good relationships'—makes a good deal of sense as a set of guiding principles for today's criminal justice system; and further, that this set of principles is capable of being translated into practice[2].

An initial observation about the concept Relational justice is that it intriguingly brings together two ideas with very different affective connotations. Justice, as J R Lucas (1980, pp 4-5) has pointed out, 'is a cold virtue'; and indeed it sometimes requires the deliberate setting aside of emotion and personal relationships, in order to seek to make what we (significantly) call a *dispassionate* judgment. By way of example, I recently acted as an external assessor in a competition for a professorship in a British university other than my own: as it happened, I already knew all of the five shortlisted candidates to varying degrees, and had worked with or taught three of them, but all these prior relationships had to be laid on one side for the purpose of trying to do justice on the occasion in question. By contrast, the idea of a 'relationship', at least when applied in human contexts, normally has an affectively warm connotation (though the warmth may sometimes be that of anger rather than friendship or love): hence, the language of emotion, care, affective ties, and the like will, without any doubt, be much more in evidence when we talk about people's relationships than when we talk about doing justice.

The juxtaposition of these two very different ideas, one affectively cold, one affectively warm, in the single proposed concept of Relational justice is, to say the least, interesting. Does the juxtaposition make any sense? And, if it does, can this be of value for our thinking about criminal justice policy?

Relational injustice?

We can usefully begin by reminding ourselves of some of the issues that arose in the days when the so-called 'rehabilitative ideal' was of central importance in some spheres of penal policy (see, *inter alia*, Allen 1964, 1981; Bottoms and Preston 1980). The rehabilitative ideal, as its name implies, especially stressed the importance of rehabilitating the offender, often using relationship-based approaches, either of a scientific kind (eg group therapy) or of a 'personal influence' kind (as seen, for instance, in the intended role of the housemaster in the former borstal system for young males: see Hood 1965). All this was seen as likely to be both more *effective* and more *humanitarian* than traditional punishments: and at first sight, it seems very difficult to do other than agree wholeheartedly with the emphasis of the rehabilitative ideal on 'good relationships' and on 'improving offenders' (apparently to everyone's benefit, including their own). However, as C S Lewis (1953) shrewdly pointed out forty years ago, at least in the scientific version of the rehabilitative ideal the special language of the treatment experts did 'not even employ such categories as rights or justice' (p 226: see also Mathiesen 1965); hence there was a danger that one might

> start being 'kind' to people before you have considered their rights, and then force upon them supposed kindnesses which they in fact had a right to refuse, and finally kindnesses which no-one but you will recognise as kindnesses and which the recipient will feel as abominable cruelties (Lewis 1953, p 230).

In case anyone thinks this is far-fetched, let me offer some real-life examples. In the 1960s in England it was by no means uncommon for probation officers, in their social enquiry reports (as they were than called) for the court, to recommend that young offenders be sent to borstal or to approved school (normally for at least nine months) rather than to detention centre (normally for only a few weeks), on the ground that the former were positive, rehabilitation-oriented training institutions, and the latter was punitive. The seriousness of the offence, and the offender's record, usually played some part, but by no means necessarily a decisive part, in reaching such recommendations. In a very similar way, in a famous small piece of research on American juvenile court judges during the heyday of the rehabilitative ideal, Stanton Wheeler and his colleagues (1968) found that judges with more liberal social and political attitudes, and a 'humanistic, social welfare ideology' (p 55), actually ordered a greater degree of intervention in the lives of those adjudged delinquent than did more socially conservative judges—and they did so because they thought that, in doing so, they were doing good.

The kind of thinking that lay behind some of these kinds of penal practice was neatly summed up in a passage of a 1960s book on English juvenile justice policy, which I could not quite believe when I originally reviewed the book, and still cannot quite believe a quarter of a century later:

> [One] objection that has been voiced is that the shift from the concept of crime, punishment and responsibility, which is endemic in the juvenile court system, to that of treatment based wholly on the needs of the offender, is to be deplored. Two adherents (Cavenagh and Sparks 1965) of the juvenile court system . . . put it thus: 'In practice the concepts of criminal responsibility and punishment have an important function: for they *limit* what can be done to offenders in the interests of justice and individual liberty' . . . As to [this] criticism . . . , it must be said that the whole purpose of the [proposed new non-court-based treatment procedure] is to concentrate on treatment needs, *and therefore what is done for a child is done in the interests of his welfare* (Boss 1967, pp 90-91, emphasis added).

Against this kind of paternalistic arrogance, albeit delivered in the name of 'welfare' or 'relationships', one clearly needs to erect some safeguards[3]. And here it is important to remember the title of one of the first and most significant critiques of the 'rehabilitative ideal': *Struggle for Justice* (American Friends Service Committee 1971). Particularly in England, commentators often seem to believe that the 'rehabilitative ideal' lost its former position of influence simply because of a powerful empirical critique: that is, research studies showed that treatment often did not have the intended rehabilitative effects (see eg Lipton, Martinson and Wilks 1975; Brody 1976). That empirical critique was, undoubtedly, part of the story. But there was also another critique, a strong theoretical one rooted in the concept of justice, and summed up in this devastating sentence from *Struggle for Justice*:

> . . . [there is] compelling evidence that the individualized treatment model, the ideal towards which reformers have been urging us for at least a century, is theoretically faulty, systematically discriminatory in administration, and inconsistent with justice (American Friends Service Committee 1971, p 12).

This is not the place to elaborate these criticisms; suffice it to say that they included the following points

—'accepted correctional practice is dominated by indoctrination in white Anglo-Saxon middle class values' (p 43)

—'the discretionary power granted to . . . judges and administrators [including parole boards] in an individualized treatment system is awesome in scope', and, because such a system postulates that each individual case must be dealt with on its particular facts and needs, 'standards are necessarily non-existent or so vague as to be meaningless, and review by any sort of court or appellate process is impossible' (p 45).

The strength of these various arguments, taken together, is very difficult to resist. In promoting 'relationalism' (if that is what we choose to do), we must not re-create some of the injustices (well-intentioned injustices, but injustices nonetheless) that occurred in the heyday of the rehabilitative ideal. As John Rawls (1972, p3) rightly said, 'justice is the *first* virtue of social institutions' (emphasis added): hence, whatever else happens, we had better try to ensure that our criminal justice system is just.

Justice and injustice

But what *is* 'justice' in a criminal justice system?

At first sight, this seems to be an impossibly daunting question: after all, human beings have been arguing about 'justice' at least since the time of Socrates, and we seem no nearer to agreed solutions. But the question gets less daunting, and easier to apply in everyday criminal justice contexts, if we follow another insight of J R Lucas (1980). For Lucas, justice is an *asymmetric* concept: it is very difficult to specify with precision what justice is, but it is much easier to identify *injustice* (and, adds Lucas, though justice is necessarily a cold virtue—see above—injustices are things that those on the receiving end often get quite warm about!)[4].

If we adopt this approach, then perhaps we can begin to specify a number of potential injustices, that one should seek to avoid, in different parts of the criminal justice system. Such potential injustices will, of necessity, vary according to which element of the overall system is being considered—for example, there will be some different kinds of possible injustice in the separate areas of discretion to prosecute, prison regimes, and the parole system. If we concentrate, by way of example, on the sentencing system, then at least the following potential injustices can perhaps be identified:

(i) Too much punishment for the offence ('no bicycle theft, however valuable the bike, deserves more than x').

(ii) Too little punishment for the offence, or complete impunity for the offender, hence an injustice to the victim and the general public ('It's outrageous that that judge let that rapist off with x').

(iii) Markedly different punishments for similar crimes committed by similar kinds of offenders ('It's awful that A got x and B got y when they did virtually the same thing . . .'); or apparently wrong rank-orderings of different offences ('How could they give C five years for that factory burglary when D only got three years for that serious assault: is property worth more than human life?').

(iv) Inhumane punishments ('How can the Saudis justify chopping off peoples' hands for theft?').

(v) Insufficient attention to the victim in the sentencing system ('Do you know, when Jill got mugged, because her attacker was pleading guilty they never even told her when the case was coming to court').

(vi) Punishment without prior just procedures ('John never got a chance to explain himself. The headmaster just expelled him without hearing his side of the story').

In the above examples, I have deliberately included some colloquial expressions of the various kinds of potential injustices, in order to illustrate that these ideas are certainly not unfamiliar ones in everyday talk about punishment and sentencing. The examples could, of course, be conceptually refined, and some at least of the possible injustices outlined might be contested, by some, as not really injustices at all[5]. But it is not my purpose, in this paper, to enter into such debates, important as they would be in their proper context. I am more concerned here simply to emphasise the main features of the preceding argument: that is to say, (i) following Lucas, we can identify justice as an asymmetric concept; and (ii) when we do this, we can quickly begin to see how talk about alleged 'injustices' incessantly permeates everyday discourse.

But if all this is right, how, amidst the welter of alleged injustices, do we identify the real injustices? Here again, I think, Lucas's discussion is helpful. Focusing as he does on *injustice*, or *unfairness*, he suggests that we think about this subjectively, and ask ourselves under what circumstances we would ourselves reasonably claim to have been treated unjustly. Colloquially, he suggests that the answer to this is when we have been 'done down' (Lucas 1980, p 5)—that is to say, when we have suffered some *unjustifiable disadvantage or disrespect at the hands of a personal agent (or agents)* (whether that agent is human or divine). Bad luck at the gambling table is not injustice; being unjustifiably treated through the malice of a bent police officer, or the culpable negligence of one's boss, is unjust. Later in his book, Lucas takes further this 'personal agency' dimension of his concept of injustice, or of being 'done down'. In thinking conceptually about justice and injustice, he argues, we should eschew impersonal conceptual schemes[6]:

> In order to justicize an action, we must either establish that any complaint of injustice is itself [factually] unjustified . . . *or adduce for deciding against a potential claimant compelling reasons of a sort whose force even he cannot evade* . . . Only then will he see that we were not acting with wanton disregard of his rights and interests, but, in spite of manifest reluctance to do him down, we still had no alternative to decide as we did. For that to be the case our reasons have to be of a special kind. They must be . . . *individualised* reasons. They must be based on facts about him, not exclusively but enough to justify, *even to him if he is reasonable,* not simply our reaching an adverse decision, but its being adverse *to him.* We have to structure the argument so that it can be seen from his point of view . . . (Lucas 1980, p 45, emphasis added).

If we follow this approach, then methodologically, when considering the possible existence of injustices in our criminal justice system—to offenders, to victims, or whoever—we need to think of ourselves as having a *conversation* with the potentially 'done down', in which his/her point of view is fully considered, and a decision adverse to him/her is reached only for reasons that he/she ought to acknowledge as cogent (see Lucas 1980, pp 67-8: though, of course, that acknowledgement might not actually be forthcoming in practice). But justice is 'concerned with everybody' in society, and not just with the underdog (p 67); hence, we must potentially be able to imagine holding these personal conversations with all relevant parties. Thus, for Lucas, though justice is unavoidably a cold concept, requiring judges and others who dispense it to distance themselves from prior relevant personal relationships, yet in the dispensing of justice itself, and in the identification of justice and injustice, there is necessarily a kind of *personalised methodology* at work. 'We cannot expect [the "done down"] to enter into our reasons if they manifest scant regard for his individuality' (Lucas 1980, p 68)[7].

These ideas, it seems to me, have much to commend them: and they provide a valuable framework for practical thinking about how to avoid injustices in our criminal justice system.

Promoting legitimacy

I now want to move from the discussion about the avoidance of injustice into some consideration of a closely connected topic, but one curiously neglected in mainstream criminology: that of *legitimacy*.

Let me begin with one more quotation from Lucas, pinpointing the connection between the avoidance of injustices and the promotion of legitimacy: even as basically good citizens, Lucas argues, we can 'have little loyalty to any institution or [social] arrangement which we regard as basically unjust' (Lucas 1980, p 5). This point is well illustrated in Thomas Mathiesen's (1965) classic study of a Norwegian correctional institution, where justice was found to be one of the main preoccupations of the prisoners, and the staff were perceived by inmates as having a great deal of power (interestingly described as *illegitimate patriarchialism*: p 101ff) over those minutiae of everyday life which become so important when one is in captivity. Even well-behaved inmates in the institution could on occasion view the regime as permeated with injustice, as in the case of prisoner Pedersen:

> To some extent, Pedersen was on very good terms with staff members, and he behaved well. However, at times he quarrelled with senior staff. For example, he was once enraged by the fact that he was not given a furlough which he felt he had a right to . . . Pedersen did not appeal to formal, written norms. Rather, he appealed to less formal but widely recognized principles of justice. For example, he criticized staff vociferously for not rewarding those who behaved well, and for deviating from the principle of equality. One of his standard phrases was 'There is so much negligence', by which he clearly implied that the staff did not stick to established principles (Mathiesen 1965, pp 13-14).

Similarly, Lord Justice Woolf, in his landmark report following the 1990 prison disturbances at Manchester and elsewhere, found that the sense of injustice among prisoners had been an important background factor in the incidents:

> A recurring theme in the evidence from prisoners who may have instigated, and who were involved in, the riots was that their actions were a response to the manner in which they were treated by the prison system. Although they did not always use these terms, they felt a lack of justice. If what they say is true, the failure of the Prison Service to fulfil its responsibilities to act with justice created in April 1990 serious difficulties in maintaining security and control in prisons (1991: para 9.24).

In the concluding paragraphs of his report, having made many suggestions for the enhancement of justice in the prison system, Lord Justice Woolf crisply re-stated his belief that *'the achievement of justice will itself enhance security and control'* (Woolf 1991, para 14.437). Elsewhere, Richard Sparks and I have argued that implicit in Woolf's report is a theory of legitimacy, that is to say, he believes that there are variable conditions in prison regimes which make it more or less likely that prisoners will accept (however conditionally) the authority of their custodians, and that a crucial element of these variable conditions will be how just are the prison conditions and the regime of the custodians (see generally Sparks and Bottoms 1995).

There is empirical evidence from an important study by Tyler (1990) to support Woolf's view that enhanced legitimacy may produce a greater compliance with legal rules; and Tyler's evidence further shows that the way in which subjects are treated by law enforcement personnel may be of particular importance in enhancing or diminishing a sense of legitimacy. The general implication of this evidence, as Tyler forcefully points out, is that those who believe that people obey the law only for reasons of self-interest (ie so-called 'instrumental compliance') are mistaken. There are alternative reasons for legal compliance which are *normative* rather than *instrumental;* and this *normative compliance* itself can be subdivided into that based on *personal morality* and that based on the *perceived legitimacy of the state authorities* (the distinction between these last two may be easily grasped by noting that in Nazi-occupied countries during the Second World War, many citizens with high moral standards felt no compunction in breaking the law, since they accorded no legitimacy to the rulers).

The potential importance of these issues in a criminological context is becoming increasingly apparent. In research on community service orders in Scotland, Gill McIvor (1992) has shown that offenders, not surprisingly, had different views as to the value of the C S experience to them, depending on the exact nature of the placement. The main reasons for valuing a placement were (i) that the offender was acquiring a new skill; (ii) that the placement offered a good deal of contact with the beneficiaries of the work (ie *relationships* with beneficiaries could be established); and (iii) that the work done could be seen as being of direct benefit to the recipient (ie the point of the work could be clearly seen, and perceived to be of *social value*). Of these three reasons, only the first could be described as instrumental, from the offender's perspective. Yet valued placements, *of any sort,* tended to lead to enhanced compliance with the terms of the community service order (ie in part, enhanced legitimacy led to compliance); and there was at least tentative evidence also that those who had attended placements that they valued had subsequently lower reoffending rates. Several offenders, too, continued to attend voluntarily at their work placements, even after completing their formal orders: in doing so, they were, quite literally, 'voting with their feet' to say that the work was truly valuable to them.

Hence, in this research project, some kinds of work placement seemed more able to command offenders' assent, and even loyalty, than did others; and similar findings can be adduced in respect of prison regimes (Sparks and Bottoms 1995). On the face of it, it seems obviously sensible, in the light of results such as these, to recommend to those in charge of penal treatments of various kinds that they should seek to promote legitimacy as one of the aims of their prison, probation team, or whatever. Before jumping to this conclusion, however, one or two potential objections must be considered.

First, is there a danger that 'promoting legitimacy' could be seen as really 'promoting softness'? Empirical evidence suggests that this is not a serious problem: for example, in McIvor's (1992) research, legitimacy was achieved in some work placements despite rigorous and demanding work. Again, in my own (so far unpublished) research project on intermediate treatment (IT) for juvenile offenders, attendance at intensive IT 'alternative to custody' projects, involving quite major inroads into offenders' weekly leisure time, was in general perceived by both offenders and their parents as significantly more helpful and constructive than was experience in 'straight' supervision orders, which made far fewer demands on offenders and their time.

Secondly, is there a danger that an emphasis on legitimacy in the eyes of offenders could be seen as 'simply about pleasing wrongdoers'? This is an important question raising complex issues about the exact nature of legitimacy, and Richard Sparks and I have discussed it in detail elsewhere (Sparks and Bottoms 1995, drawing on the work of David Beetham 1991). Suffice it to say here that the objection can be dealt with; and that, ultimately, legitimacy is not about 'pleasing wrongdoers', but about ensuring that those in authority act in accordance with the shared moral beliefs of the society in question. Thus, inmate Pedersen's dominant theme—see above—was that the prison staff were not sticking to well-established moral standards and principles of justice; where that is the case, the relevant authorities will not only tend to lose their legitimacy in the eyes of those subject to their rule, but will also ultimately be vulnerable to critique from elsewhere. Criticisms not based in shared moral beliefs, however, will carry much less weight.

Thirdly, the emphasis above has been on legitimacy in the eyes of offenders—does that mean that a penal system's legitimacy in the eyes of others (eg victims, the general public) does not matter? The answer to this is emphatically in the negative for, as we have seen, legitimacy is closely linked to the concept of justice, and we must strive to do justice (or avoid injustice) *to everyone* in society.

Given the above, it would I think make sense if penal theorists were specifically to include as part of their formulations of the General Justifying Aim of sentencing (on which see Hart 1968, ch 1), the goal of *'being part of a legitimate and legitimated criminal justice system'*, as well as whatever other goals they had in mind[8]. If that were done, it might in my view also help to make better sense of the old conundrum about whether, ultimately, one can deliver just punishments within a given society, if the social arrangements of that society appear to be fundamentally unjust.

To shed a little more light on this issue, let us consider the recent work of Lawrence Sherman (1992) on domestic violence. Sherman and his colleagues carried out a series of randomised experiments on the treatment of domestic violence by the police. In the first study, in Minneapolis, it was found that immediate arrest of the offender produced significantly better results (in terms of subsequent behaviour) than did the alternative interventions (essentially, mediation/advice, or sending the assailant away from home for a few hours). Later replications of the experiment in some cases confirmed this result, but in some cases did not. In trying to make sense of this variegated pattern of results, it eventually became clear that *the social context* in which the interventions took place was of very great importance: and the 'arrest' response, while effective in communities where assailants had strong social bonds, *actually increased domestic violence among people who had nothing to lose.* It is perhaps a reasonable interpretation of these results that where social conditions and/or the criminal justice system are basically perceived as legitimate, deterrent interventions are more likely to be effective; but where social conditions and/or the criminal justice system are such that they attract little loyalty from subjects, and are perhaps seen as oppressive and unjust, then deterrent interventions will be less effective, and might even be counterproductive. Moreover, and taking the argument a step further, perhaps in social conditions where *social justice* seems non-existent, then the legitimacy of the criminal justice system ebbs away; and, as its legitimacy ebbs, so do important aspects of its effectiveness. Legitimacy, in short, may be the crucial issue which links criminal justice and social justice. If that is so, then to promote, as part of the General Justifying Aim of sentencing, the goal of 'being part of a legitimate and legitimated criminal justice system' (see above) will also require attention to the justice of the social arrangements within which that criminal justice system is placed.

Adding a Relational dimension

I have so far argued that the goals of the criminal justice system should include the avoidance of injustice and the promotion of legitimacy. But should one go further, as proposed by the Jubilee Policy Group, and add a further factor of 'promoting relationships'?

There are good reasons for believing that one should, because of the increasing evidence of the importance of *informal social bonds* in helping to inhibit criminality. A recent and very important analysis by Sampson and Laub (1993), based on a reanalysis of data collected in the early post-war years by Sheldon and Eleanor Glueck, makes this point strongly. Briefly, Sampson and Laub's analysis showed that, in adolescence, individual difference constructs and structural background features (such as poverty) were potentially important in generating criminal behaviour, *but that they were crucially mediated through processes of informal social control in (especially) families and schools.* Moreover, after someone has become identified as a delinquent, it does not follow that he/she will always remain one—informal social bonds remain very important:

> Consistent with a sociological theory of adult development and informal social control, . . . we found that job stability and marital attachment in adulthood were significantly related to changes in adult crime—the stronger the adult ties to work and family, the less crime and deviance occurred . . . Despite differences in early childhood experiences, adult social bonds to work and family had similar consequences for the life trajectories of the 500 [identified juvenile] delinquents and 500 controls [ie non-delinquents in adolescence]. In fact, the parameter estimates of informal social control were at times nearly identical across the two groups . . . (Sampson and Laub 1993, p 248).

These results are highly congruent with the results from the Harvard research following the Massachusetts juvenile deinstitutionalisation programme of the 1970s (see Coates, Miller and Ohlin 1977), where programmes which emphasised the building of positive informal social ties were found to be more successful in preventing recidivism than were more 'closed' and inward-focused community project programmes (referred to by the authors as 'institutionalised' community programmes). The results are also consistent with some later work in the Massachusetts adult prison system, where a conscious programme of community reintegration for inmates was developed, and 'participation in the reintegration model is associated with reduced recidivism even when selection factors are controlled' (Le Clair 1988). These and other similar findings have been summarised by Kevin Haines (1990), in an important review of the literature, where the specific focus was on after-care following imprisonment. As he summarised the matter:

> . . . if a released prisoner returns to a social situation . . . in which there are few normative controls on behaviour, or a social situation (eg homelessness plus unemployment) in which the rewards are so few and the needs so high that there is little incentive to remain law abiding, then it is not surprising that the individual may commit further offences (Haines 1990, p 35).

There are good grounds, then, for emphasising the promotion of relationships within our penal treatments, in order to enhance the likelihood of reducing reoffending. One might also make the point that there is a second strong reason for arguing for an emphasis on relationships within penal treatments: namely that if relationships between staff and offenders are good, and if staff are genuinely emphasising the importance of the offender's informal social links (often very important to him/her), then legitimacy is likely to be enhanced.

But here we come back full circle to where this chapter began. In emphasising relationships, we must not do so to an extent that will create injustice, as was done in the heyday of the 'rehabilitative ideal'; nor, in a context of restricted resources, does there seem to be any strong case for promoting a relationship-based approach for *every* offender, for example where the likelihood of reoffending is in any event very low.

It was with these kinds of consideration in mind that, a few years ago, I proposed a 'mixed model' for non-custodial sentences, the essence of which is set out in *Figure 1*.

Figure 1: A Possible Framework for Sentencing with some Relational Justice Overtones

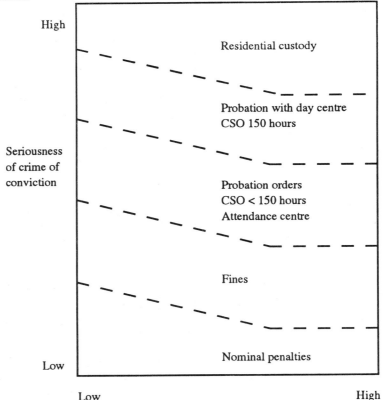

Source: Bottoms (1989), p 100

64

Essentially, my view is that the *avoidance of injustice* (see earlier section) requires the adoption of at least some features of a desert-based approach to sentencing: the potential injustices in a sentencing system listed earlier in this paper are real ones, and only an approach that emphasises, for example, like penalties for like crimes can avoid these injustices. However, it does not follow that offenders who have committed like crimes should necessarily receive *identical* sentences, so long as the amount of intervention in their lives is roughly equal. So, for example, one might have two offenders, who have committed offences judged to be, overall, of equal gravity, but from very different social circumstances:

Offender A, whose actual offence is slightly the more serious, has no previous convictions and comes from a stable social background with good informal relationships and a steady job; his likelihood of reoffending is assessed (using the best available objective indices of risk of reoffending) as low;

Offender B, whose offence is slightly less serious, has several previous convictions, so overall his current offence is judged as equal in gravity to that of Offender A[9]. Offender B comes from a multiply disadvantaged background, with many relationship problems; and his risk of reoffending is adjudged as high.

The logic of the approach to justice, and to relationships, that I have been developing in this chapter would apply to these two cases as follows. First, given that their offending is of similar gravity, injustice will be done if the penalties awarded are very different in overall severity. Secondly, however, there is clearly a good case for paying more attention to relationships in B's case than in A's. Within the logic of *Figure 1* (see the second band in the figure) it would not be inappropriate to award A, say, a long community service order, and B a probation order incorporating an intensive 'probation centre' condition. Space does not permit any further exploration of this—but it can reasonably be argued that the line of thinking is in fact embodied, in England and Wales, in section 6(2) Criminal Justice Act 1991, which requires sentencers, when ordering community penalties, to have regard *both* to whether the restrictions on liberty imposed by the order or orders are commensurate with the seriousness of the offence(s), *and* to whether the order (or orders) is 'the most suitable' for the offender, in his/her particular situation (which must presumably include some consideration of his/her relationships).

Conclusion

I began this chapter by pointing out that justice is an affectively cold concept, while relationships are affectively warm; and also that, as we saw in the heyday of the rehabilitative ideal, if we are not careful then an emphasis on relationships can promote injustices. But I have tried to argue, too, that the *avoidance of injustice,* the *promotion of legitimacy* and the *promotion of relationships* all make sense as major goals for a criminal justice system, the last of these on the dual grounds of probable reductions in reoffending and probable enhancements of legitimacy. If all this is accepted, the crucial point, I would argue, is that all three of the goals should be kept in balance, so that one does not dominate at the expense of the others; and, following Rawls, I would myself particularly emphasise the primacy of justice within this trio of concepts.

I would finally reiterate that, in my view, all three of the key concepts used in this chapter are capable of being employed by criminal justice practitioners in their thinking about day-to-day practices: hence, in different contexts, the prison governor, the probation officer and the sentencer can all usefully reflect on how 'avoiding injustice, and promoting legitimacy and relationships' might optimally be translated into practice in their own particular spheres of responsibility. But to attempt to exemplify this claim in any detail would require another paper.

Notes

1 The Jubilee Policy Group's overall aim is to promote a 'Christian analysis of public policy'. It is not a secret that I am myself interested in the application of Christian theology to criminal justice issues (see Bottoms and Preston 1980), but I have not attempted any explicitly theological analysis in this chapter. Those with an interest in such matters will, however, find some continuities in approach between what is said in this chapter and the concluding chapter of the Bottoms/Preston collection (written jointly by Michael Taylor and myself)

2 I do wish to place on record how very stimulating I have found the proposed concept of 'Relational Justice'; the formulation that I now propose would almost certainly not have been developed in this way had the Jubilee Group not engaged me in a number of conversations about the topic.

3 There is a theological dimension that is worth noting here: as C S Lewis (1953, p 226) put it, views such as that in the quoted passage imply 'a simple-minded view of fallen human nature'. See also Home Office Prison Department (1983, pp 23-24).

4 It is worth pointing out that, in my view at least, influential modern approaches to sentencing such as those of Norval Morris and Andrew von Hirsch are consistent with Lucas's view of the asymmetric character of the concept of justice: this point is discussed in Bottoms (1994).

5 Most notably by utilitarians: see generally Walker (1991)

6 Here and elsewhere, Lucas's language is strikingly non-gender-inclusive.

7 For Lucas (1980, p 68), 'this is what vitiated utilitarianism. It made no concession to the individual, treating him only as a unit; and in submerging his pay-off in an anonymous sum total, it was, in effect, inviting him to merge his individuality in a collective whole'. Lucas similarly argues that Rawls's (1972) methodology, in the famous 'original position', is insufficiently 'a dialogue with *actual persons* who are *actually worst off*' (Lucas 1980, p 194, emphasis added).

8 In the work of different penal theorists, these goals differ somewhat: they virtually always include the prevention of crime, and, depending on the theorist, they may also include other aims (see eg von Hirsch 1993, ch 2).

9 This assumes that prior convictions add some weight to the seriousness of the current offence, an approach best conceptualised theoretically in terms of a 'progressive loss of mitigation': see Ashworth (1992, pp 147-50)

References

Allen, F A (1964) *The Borderland of Criminal Justice* (Chicago: University of Chicago Press)

Allen, F A (1981) *The Decline of the Rehabilitative Ideal* (New Haven: Yale University Press)

American Friends Service Committee (1971) *Struggle for Justice: A Report on Crime and Punishment in America* (New York: Hill and Wang)

Ashworth, A J (1992) *Sentencing and Criminal Justice* (London: Weidenfeld and Nicolson)

Beetham, D (1991) *The Legitimation of Power* (London: Macmillan)

Boss, P (1967) *Social Policy and the Young Delinquent* (London: Routledge and Kegan Paul)

Bottoms, A E (1989) 'The concept of intermediate sanctions and its relevance for the probation service', in R Shaw and K Haines (Eds) *The Criminal Justice System: A Central Role for the Probation Service* (Cambridge: Institute of Criminology)

Bottoms, A E (1994) 'The philosophy and politics of punishment and sentencing' in C Clarkson and R Morgan (Eds) *The Politics of Sentencing* (Oxford: Clarendon Press)

Bottoms, A E and Preston, R H (Eds) (1980) *The Coming Penal Crisis: A Criminological and Theological Exploration* (Edinburgh: Scottish Academic Press)

Brody, S (1976) *The Effectiveness of Sentencing*, Home Office Research Study No 35 (London: HMSO)

Cavenagh, W E and Sparks, R F (1965) 'Out of court', *New Society*, 6, No 146, p 9

Coates, R B, Miller, A D and Ohlin, L E (1977) *Diversity in a Youth Correctional System* (Cambridge, Mass: Ballinger)

Haines, K (1990) *After-Care Services for Released Prisoners: A Review of the Literature* (Cambridge: Institute of Criminology)

Hart, H L A (1968) *Punishment and Responsibility* (Oxford: Oxford University Press)

Home Office Prison Department (1983) *Working Party on Regimes for Dangerously Disruptive Prisoners Report* (London: Home Office Prison Department, Chaplain-General's Office)

Hood, R (1965) Borstal Reassessed (London: Heinemann Educational Books)

Le Clair, D (1988) *The Effect of Community Reintegration on Rates of Recidivism: A Statistical Overview of Data for the Years 1971 Through 1985* (Massachusetts: Massachusetts Department of Corrections)

Lewis, C S (1953) 'The humanitarian theory of punishment' *Res Judicatae*, 6, 224-230.

Lipton, D, Martinson, R and Wilks, J (1975) *The Effectiveness of Correctional Treatment* (New York: Praeger)

Lucas, J R (1980) *On Justice* (Oxford: Clarendon Press)

Mathiesen, T (1965) *The Defences of the Weak* (London: Tavistock Publications)

McIvor, G (1992) *Sentenced to Serve* (Aldershot: Avebury)

Rawls, J (1972) *A Theory of Justice* (London: Oxford University Press)

Sampson, R J and Laub, J H (1993) *Crime in the Making*, (Cambridge, Mass: Harvard University Press)

Schluter, M and Lee, D (1993) *The R-Factor* (London: Hodder and Stoughton)

Sherman, L W (1992) *Policing Domestic Violence: Experiments and Dilemmas* (New York: Free Press)

Sparks, R and Bottoms, A E (1995) 'Legitimacy and order in prisons', *British Journal of Sociology* (forthcoming).

Tyler, T R (1990) *Why People Obey the Law* (New Haven: Yale University Press)

von Hirsch, A (1993) *Censure and Sanctions* (Oxford: Clarendon Press)

Walker, N D (1991) *Why Punish?* (Oxford: Oxford University Press)

Wheeler, S, Bonacich, E, Cramer, M R and Zola, I K (1968) 'Agents of delinquency control' in S Wheeler (Ed) *Controlling Delinquency* (New York: John Wiley)

Woolf, Lord Justice (1990) *Prison Disturbances, April 1990*, Cm 1456 (London: HMSO)

Part II

Applying Relational Justice

CHAPTER 5

Mediation, Reparation and Justice

Nicola Baker

A woman and her eight year old son were the victims of an aggravated burglary, in which they were terrorised by the burglar. He received a prison sentence. The boy's nightmares persisted and as time drew near for the burglar to be released the woman became apprehensive that the burglar would return. She approached her local advice centre, who referred her to the local Mediation and Reparation Service.[1]

The mediators visited the offender who had just been released. He was upset to hear that his victim was still so worried. A meeting was arranged at the advice centre, at which the offender apologised in full and reassured the victim that he had no intention of returning to cause harm. The victim accepted the apology and reassurance, and said that she found the meeting helpful. The boy's nightmares stopped soon afterwards.

A story like this demonstrates how crime damages human relationships. The central relationship created by crime is that between the offender and the victim and, if this is not addressed, the damage persists even though the offender has been punished. Relationships are not absent even between strangers for 'whether or not they ever meet, the offender and the victim are locked into a relationship. Without knowing each other in reality, they know each other intimately in their imaginations.'[2] In the case outlined above, the victims were given an opportunity to meet their burglar and resolve their anxieties. Such a meeting is still a rarity within our present criminal justice system.

The circumstances of many offences make any further contact between victim and offender extremely painful if not completely inappropriate. Naturally, victims are often reluctant to meet the individual who harmed them. Because most crimes do not result in a criminal conviction, the vast majority of victims never have identifiable offenders. Likewise, crimes may have corporate rather than individual victims. Why therefore would Relational Justice advocate extending the use of mediation and reparation to bring together victims and offenders in an effort to reconcile them?

Mediation and reparation embody in principle and in practice the core values of Relational Justice. They share the same starting point, that the victim and the offender are the principal players in the drama of crime.

Relational Justice sees crime primarily in terms of a breakdown of relationships—in which violation of the state and its laws is not the only consideration. Achieving justice becomes more than simply punishing the wrong-doer: it is about putting right the wrong. In part this means putting right the relationship between the victim and the offender. In seeking to protect victims and achieve justice for them, our present system—with its emphasis on identifying guilt or innocence—marginalises victims, by its very philosophy and practice. Victims become observers of, rather than participants in, the process of resolving 'their' crime.

More fundamentally, the system fails to address the fact that victims of crime suffer both material *and* psychological harm. Material compensation may be forthcoming but rarely can the present system offer victims healing at an emotional or spiritual level. Uniquely, victim/offender mediation opens up a variety of possibilities for achieving both material and psychological compensation for victims through a range of outcomes.

Mediation or reparation?

Mediation can be defined as: *the intervention of a third party to help two (or more) parties in conflict to communicate and, where possible and appropriate, resolve their differences and achieve a settlement.*

Mediation is a practical way of enabling parties in conflict to find their own resolution with the support of a mediator. Although increasingly a common feature of civil disputes—especially in family law suits, industrial relations cases and neighbourhood disputes—the application of mediation in criminal cases is, perhaps surprisingly, still largely unrecognised and undervalued.

Mediation can take different forms. Typically it involves the intervention of a trained mediator who aims to facilitate contact between two conflicting parties. The mediator acts as guide, referee and go-between to help the parties communicate, understand the other's position and settle their differences.

Victim/offender mediation is a process involving various stages. The mediator assesses the willingness of either party to participate before arranging a meeting. Several outcomes are possible. If the parties are unwilling to meet but wish to offer an apology or a sign of forgiveness, the mediator may help the parties draw up letters to that effect and act as a go-between. The majority of victim/offender schemes aim to achieve a face-to-face meeting and a deeper level of understanding. Ideally, some form of reconciliation should result. Many mediation schemes are set up specifically to give offenders and victims the opportunity to negotiate an appropriate form of reparation or compensation. Some schemes operate on a group basis such as the Plymouth Probation Victim/Burglar Group, where several offenders meet several victims of similar but unconnected crimes.

Mediation and reparation are often discussed together. But it is helpful to view them separately. Mediation can often lead to reparation—and ideally it does—but this does not always happen. By the same token, reparation of some kind can be imposed by the courts even though no mediation has taken place.

A definition of reparation might be: *action by the offender to make good the loss suffered by the victim.*

'Making good' is obviously a wide definition encompassing both tangible and intangible forms of reparation. This reflects the nature and extent of the harm done, both material and psychological. Take the case of a dispute between neighbours over a broken fence. Appropriate material compensation could be achieved if the fence were to be replaced by the perpetrator. But psychological reparation might require him or her to make a full written apology or perhaps to pay for the repair of the fence—or even to carry out repairs in person.

Material compensation can never fully replace the loss of objects of great sentimental value such as a wedding ring or an antique heirloom, but an offender can make a genuine gesture of remorse. If the burglar who stole my jewellery had been caught, I would have asked him to plant bulbs in my garden to remind me each year of the items which had been important to me. Whether the offender is able to pay back the full value of the loss incurred or only a token amount, reparation reinforces the relational dimension of an offence. Sometimes reparation may not benefit the victim directly but may involve compensation to the community (though possibly at the victim's request) in the form eg of a community service order helping in a day centre for disabled children or fixing security locks to properties on vulnerable estates.

But reparation is more than mere compensation. One criticism of compensation orders has been that many victims feel insulted by the assumption that money can put right the whole wrong that they have suffered. Victims need both the material and the psychological effects of crime to be resolved; frequently, receiving a sincere apology is more satisfying to a victim than financial compensation alone. Mediation therefore plays a unique role within the criminal justice process because it not only aims to address the parties' needs directly but also makes the achievement of some reconciliation at the psychological level a *primary* aim.

Mediation—who benefits?

A decade ago concern was frequently expressed that the *offender* based focus of many victim/offender mediation schemes was compromising the essence of mediation as an impartial service. This was the chief reason why victim support groups had been wary of extending the practice of mediation. Today, mediation and reparation schemes are seen to provide balanced, if different, benefits for victims and offenders. Even where the aim is diversion from the court process, schemes cannot be accused of offender 'bias' if victims' needs are also being properly addressed.

Referrals to mediation can be accepted at any stage in the criminal justice process, whether on behalf of the victim or the offender, thereby preserving an even-handed approach. First contact is however more likely to be made with the offender. Mediation can be offered:

(a) as a result of a referral following a police caution, possibly in conjunction with the decision of an out of court youth justice panel hearing, particularly where diversion is a main objective;

(b) if prosecution is for some reason discontinued or deferred;

(c) pre-trial, perhaps as a result of a victim offering to participate;

(d) post-conviction but prior to sentencing on the advice of a probation officer or defence lawyer or, although rarely, by the judge at the sentencing stage where placement on a mediation scheme is made part of a probation order;

(e) post-sentence, whilst serving, or after completing, a sentence, where an offender realises that he or she has failed to make amends.

Benefits to the offender can result from mediation, the most significant being the opportunity that mediation gives to demonstrate the acceptance of responsibility for the harm done and to make amends to the victim. Many offenders experience real release from feelings of remorse and guilt having faced up to the consequences of their actions and having done what they can to cover the loss. For some it may well have been the first time that they were made aware of the personal suffering they caused to another human being by their actions: the trauma to children caused by a damaged toy, the fear generated by intrusion of privacy experienced by a victim—out of all proportion to the actual physical damage or financial loss incurred.

It is the power of the face-to-face contact between an offender and his or her victim which creates the dynamic for potential change in both parties, in a way that a court appearance and imprisonment frequently fail to achieve. On hearing for the first time the victim's side of the story, the offender's defensive strategy of 'neutralising' his or her actions by denying responsibility, or the level of seriousness of the offence, is undermined. No longer can a burglar find inner comfort by saying 'they're insured', 'they'll never miss it' or 'we were only having fun' when confronted with a mother's story of her sobbing child or a student whose thesis material, representing several years' work, has vanished with the computer. Face-to-face meetings bring about a human dimension and give a personality to both victim and offender. They break down stereotypical attitudes: 'these are only rich middle class people who don't know what life is like for the rest of us'.

Imprisonment, on the other hand, often only encourages the tendency of offenders to 'neutralise' their offences by removing them from the human consequences of their actions and thereby shielding them from the pain of confronting reality.

Sometimes the mediation process highlights and creates opportunities to deal with underlying factors which contributed to the offender's conduct. An offender who has difficulty in relating to adults because of poor parenting can be deeply affected by receiving a victim's forgiveness, opening up new possibilities for trust.

Where mediation results in a reduced sentence or the avoidance of prison, there are benefits not only to the offender but also to his or her family as important relationships and community ties can be maintained. To the extent that these ties deter from future offending, the community can also see a benefit.

Critics of mediation and reparation have argued that successful outcomes should not be allowed to serve as mitigation affecting sentence, thereby preventing an offender from receiving his or her 'just deserts'. They consider that this could give such offenders an unfair advantage.

Certainly mitigation should never be the exclusive aim of mediation. But a process, whether it is seen as punitive or not, which results in genuine remorse and acceptance of responsibility on the part of an offender, does achieve one of the primary objectives of punishment. In some cases, successful mediation may result in a higher tariff response where the court recognises an offender's additional responsibility to his or her victim.[3]

I believe that, if mediation and reparation were to be offered to all victims and offenders as the rule rather than the exception, the perception of unfair advantage would diminish as cases of legitimate mitigation become more common.

For victims, mediation provides a structured environment to vent feelings of bitterness and hurt directly to the one who caused them. Victims of crime experience feelings of helplessness, anger, fear, and loss of confidence. To meet the offender and to ensure that they are not going to repeat the offence, may alleviate some of the fears and help the victim readjust to normal life.

Meeting the offender gives the victim the opportunity to ask questions like: 'Why me?', 'What happened to my jewellery?', 'Had you been watching the house?' and to learn the offender's side of the story.

The most obvious benefit to victims from mediation is the opportunity to agree a form of reparation which they feel adequately compensates for the harm caused to them.

Moreover, it gives the victim a chance to extend forgiveness. The act of forgiving can, more than any intervention by the criminal justice system, allow the victim to put a closure on the whole experience.

Mediation —how effective?

Existing mediation and reparation schemes have faced a number of difficulties in quantifying their benefits to the satisfaction of policy makers and funders. These obstacles, compounded by the shortage of detailed research and analysis of outcomes, have left mediation on the margins of the present criminal justice process with many questions about its efficacy.

There are at present some 25 different services offering victim/offender mediation and reparation in England and Wales, two in Scotland. They vary in objectives and procedures and this makes comparison of their merits at different stages, and for different offenders and offences, problematic. Mediation schemes whose primary aim is reparation cannot be compared with those aiming to divert from the criminal justice process via reparation. Success may be measured very differently. In one case a victim was able to provide a job to an unemployed offender which then enabled the offender to pay back compensation. More usually, a simple letter of apology may satisfy.

In the mid-1980s, the Home Office undertook comparative research on several schemes including those which it had set up by way of experiment. Results from this study[4] showed that a high level of victim/offender meetings was achieved with agreement being reached in over 80 per cent of cases. Some positive, if slight, effect on later offending patterns was achieved with those who had face-to-face contact with their victim. Courts endorsed the positive effects on the offender by accepting the efforts made by them to atone for their crime as a factor alleviating the punishment imposed. An analysis of sentencing patterns over time showed that about one quarter of disposals were changed, between 5 per cent and 10 per cent involving a non-custodial sentence in place of a custodial one (although there were occasional cases where a higher penalty was imposed).

Similar findings in a study on Kettering Adult Reparation Bureau[5] during 1987-89 found a victim and offender satisfaction rate of 70 per cent.

Rates of reoffending were lowest for those who had taken part in face-to-face meetings with victims.

Table: Reoffending Rates at Kettering Adult Reparation Bureau				
Procedure	No of reconvictions (%)			
	0	1	2	3+
Face-to-face (bureau)	84.6	10.8	3.1	1.5
Go-between (bureau)	78.4	12.2	1.4	8.0
Court	80.0	10.7	4.0	5.3

Source: Northamptonshire Adult Reparation Bureau Review 1986-1993

Although attempts have been made to measure the cost-effectiveness of schemes, such assessments remain speculative. It can never be assumed that a particular alternative disposal would have been imposed if mediation or reparation had failed. Nor is it possible to accurately value non-financial consequences such as the amount of hurt which is healed.

At Kettering, cost savings of £600 per case have been calculated yielding a notional annual saving in 1992/3 of £233,600 over the 791 successful diversion cases in 1992.[6] Magistrates courts were found to benefit most[7]:

Probation	3%
Police	9%
Crown Prosecution Service	10%
Criminal legal aid	38%
Magistrates courts	40%

Another significant finding from the Kettering experience is the very high percentage of completed compensation orders, nearly 97 per cent, when initiated through mediation.

A more recent study of two SACRO schemes in Edinburgh and Glasgow found that the main cost savings of mediation were made only when a custodial sentence was avoided.[8]

Mediation —integral or independent?
Much of the present debate among advocates of extending mediation and reparation revolves around the location of such schemes in relation to the criminal justice process. Purists argue that, where schemes are operating

within the present system and largely funded by existing criminal justice agencies, the objectives of the system inevitably dominate and compromise the essence of mediation, which is impartiality between victim and offender. It becomes difficult (though certainly not impossible) to maintain an even-handed approach. This is especially the case where a scheme is aiming to achieve both reparation for the victim and diversion for the offender.[9]

One solution has been to grant greater autonomy in relation to the running of mediation schemes to inter-agency management committees, thereby affording the schemes more independence to set their own objectives. Those where Victim Support are closely involved, such as the Plymouth Victim/Burglar Group, have seen the credibility of mediation enhanced—especially with victims. It is possible that moves within the probation service to make more use of outside agencies on a contract basis could lead to an expansion in mediation services which are independent of any one agency.

Other factors are fuelling interest in schemes which could operate completely outside of the formal criminal justice process Growing interest in extending the concept of 'alternative dispute resolution' beyond the civil sphere has accompanied increased public disillusionment with the ability of the present system to contend with current crime levels. Mediation UK, the umbrella body which advises on all forms of mediation in the UK, receives regular enquiries about setting up new schemes. At the same time, pressures to find less costly ways of punishing offenders may encourage further experimentation.

Experience in other countries is relevant here. For example, in Norway the network of Municipal Mediation Boards[10] is easing the burden on the courts by providing a route away from the prosecution of young or first-time offenders and achieving genuine 'alternative' status.

But without government funding—central or local—it is unlikely that community-based dispute resolution models will make a significant impact on criminal justice practice in the United Kingdom. It will take time before the track record of neighbourhood dispute centres, of which there are currently some 40-50 in existence,[11] is established and they are seen to be able to handle increasingly more serious offences.

Without the 'yeast' of the relational dynamic which mediation provides operating within mainstream justice, the 'dough' of the present system will remain unleaven. Therefore, in advocating independent schemes, there is no doubt that mediation and reparation should be offered more extensively within the present system. The multi-agency management approach should ensure professionalism and balanced benefits to both victim and offender.

Mediating justice

The more that a society relies on coercion by professional agencies to engender law-abiding behaviour, the less likely it is that communities and individuals will assume social responsibility and the more likely it is that an overall increase in fear and anonymity will result.

The concept of mediation as a model for conflict resolution—both within the current system and alongside it—sends out important signals about the principles which should underlie the process of justice in all cases. These principles are central to Relational Justice and have practical implications for the criminal justice process:

Principles

(a) *Crime concerns damaged relationships between people*
Crime is primarily an offence against a person or persons. Crime creates a relationship between victim and offender, even where none existed before. Victims are affected by crime materially and psychologically, whether the offence was personal or property-related.

• Offenders and victims should be respected as individuals not cases. Face-to-face contact in a mediated context enhances respect for persons, breaks down stereotypical attitudes, highlights the relational dimension to crime and allows the particular circumstances of the offence under consideration and the offender/victim relationship to influence the outcome.

(b) *Justice involves a fair process*
The delivery of justice should be seen to be 'fair' on all parties involved. For the victim, this means being treated with respect, not merely as fodder for the defence; for the offender, it means trying to identify and address underlying factors affecting his or her conduct.

• Parity should be maintained between a victim's and an accused person's access to the justice process so that both parties' interests are addressed in an even-handed way. Fairness is enhanced by establishing a more direct link between the offence and the punishment and by speeding up responses by the system.
• Communities and individuals should be enabled in many more instances to find their own solution to conflict. The role of the state and its agencies is to empower and facilitate parties in conflict to find their own mutually acceptable resolution rather than to impose one from outside.

(c) *Justice involves a fair outcome*

Justice can only be fully achieved when the needs of the victim of crime have been addressed and where the harm caused to the victim—both material harm and psychological harm—has been repaired in some way, in whole or in part.

• The process of justice involves arriving at a form of punishment which holds in tension both backward-looking aspects (the harm done to the victim and the punishment which is deserved) and the forward-looking aspects which anticipate repairing the breach caused by crime and reintegrating the offender into the community[12]. To have the offender face up to the consequences of his or her crime and to be challenged by the human suffering he or she caused is not a soft option. For many offenders, it is much more demanding to come face-to-face with an angry, hurting, fellow human being than rows of impersonal judicial figures acting out a seemingly irrelevant piece of theatre in a courtroom.

Practical implications

(a) *Extend the use of reparation*

Reparation, whether tangible or intangible, should be a feature of all cases and the opportunity to make amends should be offered in every appropriate case including when a custodial sentence is in prospect. Courts already have power to order monetary compensation. They should have a general power to order non-financial reparation. If making amends is seen as the responsibility of all offenders and a natural act for anyone guilty of an offence, the concern that compliance with reparation measures becomes merely a means to obtain leniency from the court is removed: reparation becomes the rule rather than the exception.

• Custodial sentences should only be used as a last resort where concerns about endangering the public sufficiently outweigh the negative effects of imprisonment on the offender's ability to take responsibility and the potentially destructive influence on family and friendship relationships and future employability. Imprisonment fails the victim as well as the offender and severely limits the opportunity to make amends.

(b) *Involve victims and communities more*

Victims should be allowed to participate in the criminal justice process. Their involvement must always remain voluntary. Victims can play a unique role which no criminal justice agency can fulfil: they can extend forgiveness.

• Involvement of 'significant others' should also be sought, those who are part of either the victim's or the offender's wider family, friends and workmates. As Braithwaite argues, the shaming process is a much more effective deterrent when it involves people whose good opinion the offender cares about, much less so if imposed by a remote legal authority.[13]

• Community members have a significant role to play in contributing to the criminal justice process as 'ordinary' citizens, not representatives of the penal establishment. Volunteer participation in the justice process lowers the barrier between the law-enforcers and the law-breakers and provides the opportunity for community values of local accountability and service for the common good to be exercised. Local communities are thereby encouraged to 'own' their responses to crime in their area, to take an interest in crime prevention and social control.

Conclusion

Mediation and reparation are important practical expressions of Relational Justice. Together they affirm the centrality of relationships in understanding and responding to crime. They embody both the spirit and the values of Relational Justice: respect for the individual within a web of relationships, parity between the interests and needs of victim and offender, and preference for face-to-face conflict resolution over the impersonal court process.

Where crime is seen as a broken relationship, mediation is a means to repairing that relationship. For the offender, the power of encounter challenges the tendency to 'neutralise' offending behaviour and shatters the stereotypical image of the victim. 'I'm sorry' is one of the hardest things to say to another human being. Mediation provides a structure which can make this easier. For the victim, it is an opportunity to address fears and anger and to begin again to lead a normal life. It has been well observed by the Greek physician Hippocrates that 'healing is a matter of time but it is sometimes also a matter of opportunity.'[14] Mediation provides that opportunity.

Notes

1 Case history supplied by Leeds Mediation and Reparation Service.

2 Marshall, T and Merry, S (1990) *Crime and Accountability: Victim/Offender Mediation in Practice*, HMSO, p 1

3 *Ibid* p 126; also Dignan, J (Autumn 1992) *Repairing the Damage: Can Reparation be Made to Work in the Service of Diversion?* British Journal of Criminology, Vol 32, No 4, p 463.

4 Marshall, T and Merry, S (1990)

5 Dignan, J (1990) *Repairing the Damage: An evaluation of an experimental adult reparation scheme in Kettering*, Centre for Criminological and Legal Research, Faculty of Law, University of Sheffield.

6 Wright, A (1986-1993) *Northamptonshire Adult Reparation Bureau Review*.

7 Dignan, J (1990)

8 Warner, S (1992) *Making Amends: Justice for Victims and Offenders*, Avebury: University of Stirling.

9 Dignan, J (1992)

10 Royal Norwegian Ministry of Justice and Police, *Municipal Mediation Boards: an alternative to prosecution*. Available via Mediation UK.

11 *Directory of Mediation & Conflict Resolution Services*, Mediation UK, May 1994.

12 Lacey, N (1988) *State Punishment: Political Principles and Community Values*. Routledge. London & New York.

13 Braithwaite, J (1989) *Crime, Shame and Reintegration*. Cambridge: Cambridge University Press.

14 *Precepts*. Cited in Partington, A (ed) (1992) *The Oxford Dictionary of Quotations*. Oxford: Oxford University Press.

CHAPTER 6

Local Justice: A Personal View

Christopher Compston

Chiswick Town Hall opened in February 1901. On 1 April 1965 the London Government Act 1963 annulled the existing pattern of local administration; Chiswick became part of the new Borough of Hounslow. As a local historian wrote, 'It is not surprising that Chiswick, bereft of civic glory and central administration from its own Town Hall, experienced some loss of identity as a community'. What of the Town Hall today in 1994? Jumble Sales, whist drives, charity fairs, even an occasional location for the television series *Crown Court!*—in short, dead as the dodo.

Strand on the Green, a hamlet between Chiswick and Kew Bridges, runs alongside the Thames towpath. Some years ago, whilst clearing rubbish from the foreshore, an elderly professor's wife remarked 'You see that new development on the old wharf site?' I looked at a row of expensive town houses, built three years before. 'Well', she continued, 'before they were built, there were about 70 houses here; I felt I knew everyone. Now, I don't. We are no longer a village and the odd thing is that I don't know the original 70 as well as I did. Somehow, it's got too big for me to handle'.

That passing remark underlines the point that, speaking simplistically, small is beautiful and big is bad. This was brilliantly expounded by E F Schumacher in his book *Small is Beautiful*, first published in 1973. We can all cope with just so much, with just so many people—our family, our friends, our fellow workers and so on, but beyond a certain size we give up. 'They' don't belong to 'us' and 'we' don't belong to 'them'.

This has great relevance to sentencing.

The need for local courts
For hundreds of years, justice in England and Wales was administered by unpaid justices of the peace sitting in local courts. Above them were Quarter Sessions, run by a recorder or chairman, sitting regularly for an intensive few days, often disposing of more cases in one day than many a modern Crown Court does in three. Above them were Assizes, presided

over by a visiting High Court judge—trumpets, the judge's lodgings, the High Sheriff with wife in a splendid hat and chaplain in full regalia—all very traditional.

The essential point is that all these courts were local, the more important the case, the larger the catchment area, nevertheless, local. The justices were the natural leaders of the large village or town—and what on earth was wrong with that? They varied but they knew the local ropes, the local people, and sentenced accordingly. A young barrister, attending East Ham magistrates' court on Monday, Overton on Tuesday, Clerkenwell on Wednesday, Reading on Thursday and Bow Street on Friday soon realised that it was 'horses for courses'. In short, Monday's mitigation would not wash with Tuesday's Bench. The East Ham docker often had a very different outlook from the retired colonel in Overton but, locally, they just about got it right.

Likewise at Quarter Sessions and Assizes. The recorder of a borough (unlike the chairman of a county Quarter Sessions) was not local. However, he almost invariably identified with the town, attended all its functions and became part of the local scene. By and large, it worked very well. Furthermore, we all lunched together on the first court day. Judge, clerk, local solicitor, probation officer and barrister identified with the place.

At Assizes, High Court judges sometimes became identified with certain counties. Even if they did not, by their meetings with local dignitaries they soon got the local flavour.

All this was destroyed by Lord Beeching—as wise with the courts as he was with British Railways? The Crown Courts began on 1 January 1972, replacing Assizes and Quarter Sessions. Over the last 20 years, courts have become increasingly large and centralised, with more power given over to the central administration and civil servants, increasingly dominated by the Treasury.

The Lord Chancellor's Department does recognise the inherent tension between what it calls 'local justice' and the pressure to 'modernise' the management structure of the courts to improve performance and accountability. However, the solution set out in the department's publication *A New Framework for Local Justice* [1] and enshrined in the Police and Magistrates' Courts Act 1994 seems to infer, to my mind, a rather different and somewhat flexible definition of 'local'. This has meant in practice combining court functions, reducing the number of administrative districts and closing some courts. Although local magistrates' courts committees still set local priorities, they must now be subject to 'guidance' from the Lord Chancellor on strategy, resourcing and 'performance' in order to achieve a 'less fragmented and parochial' magistracy.

This centralising process should be watched carefully. A public enquiry can be held on the proposed demolition of a listed building, however, derelict. But there is no public enquiry when a local court is closed or or its use is curtailed.

This point was taken up in *The Guardian* on 21 April 1994 by Andrew Phillips. In a piece entitled 'An Open and Shut Case of Injustice' he stressed that accessibility to justice is part psychological, part financial and part geographical. A local court satisfies all three of these components becoming, over time, an unintimidating part of everyone's life. As Phillips points out, a local court is cheap and easy to get to if you are a parent with a pram on family court business, a witness or a publican going along for an occasional licence, not to mention the regular attenders, such as solicitors, doctors or policemen. Now, with increasing momentum, lead by the Treasury, these courts are being closed down, regardless of cost or inconvenience to the consumer—provided the official court costs are saved. In fact, one might well question how much the Treasury actually does save, even following its narrow accounting guidelines. One witness, too old, ill, frightened, incompetent, or poor to travel the ten miles to the nearest court may well radically undermine the so called savings. Be that as it may, the financial and other costs to the public are increased. What is to be done?

The solution lies in slowing down the building of 'supermarket' courts—those *Palais de Justice*, duly opened by the Lord Chancellor in full dress, his visit commemorated by a handsome plaque. Local courts should be opened or re-opened.

There are three important exceptions. Firstly, difficult and dangerous cases warrant first rate security and facilities; a modernised court complex like the Central Criminal Court, the Old Bailey, being an admirable example. Secondly, if convicted, these criminals will receive a long prison sentence. Subject to certain conditions, a local court is less necessary. Thirdly, in civil matters, where eg insurance company is fighting insurance company and the personal element is negligible, a local court is not necessary. Incidentally, such users of the court could well pay the full cost thereof plus a subsidy to help the more vulnerable litigants. Furthermore, these cases can always be remitted to local courts when they have run out of local cases. A judge should be able to switch with ease from crime to civil to family work.

So, my premise is to retain and increase local courts, magistrates' courts, county courts and Crown Court centres to deal with the main burden of cases involving the ordinary (and the not so ordinary) citizen. These would cover crime and family matters as well as some civil matters such as landlord and tenant, neighbour disputes and personal civil actions. These courts should be easily accessible, near to car parks, banks, building societies, supermarkets and the like—in the market place, part of the community.

In passing, the Lord Chancellor's department might well consider using temporary courts, ie buildings which are courts in the day and something else in the evenings and weekends. Formerly, courts were sometimes held in the most strange of places—to no one's particular detriment. This could still be done provided the hard cases were siphoned off to secure, purpose built courts. Chiswick Town Hall, like many public buildings, could provide two courts at minimal expense. It has all the supporting facilities in place, including shops, the Underground, buses and car parks, even traffic wardens! Redundant churches could find a new purpose.

Local judges in local courts
At the moment, High Court judges spend some time on circuit and part of their time in London. For a few years they may be presiding judges of their circuit. Apparently there is a sensible plan to have them spend all of their time outside London on a circuit. They could then be responsible for all the courts and judges within their jurisdiction. This must be a good idea. On occasions, the Court of Appeal could sit outside London, thus directly benefiting the regions.

That local High Court judge should know the local judges well, both on and off the bench. Sitting in the same courts, they should meet frequently. In my five years sitting in Birmingham, the High Court judge never once joined the local circuit judges and recorders for lunch. He should have done. Recently, Lord Justice Russell from the Court of Appeal lunched at the Knightsbridge Crown Court. In his admirably down to earth way, he asked for our views on his Court and got them! To borrow George III's remark on a 'mad' general, 'Would that he would bite some of his fellow judges!'.

To digress, some years ago I lunched with John Piper, the well known painter. The least important guest, I was placed at the bottom of the table but, after the soup, he suddenly swapped places with his wife, leaving her to talk high art with the pundits and me to talk gardens with him. At Reading Crown Court, Mr Justice Woolf (now Lord Woolf), gained considerable brownie points by unexpectedly having lunch in the general canteen. Sadly, these gestures are far too rare.

The term 'judges' should be taken to include magistrates and tribunal chairmen. Often tribunals are more important to the average citizen than the courts, which they may never visit.

Outside of the large cities, judges are more local, but recent amalgamations have undermined this. Local justice is more regional than local. For instance, in 1993, the Braintree magistrate's court was closed.

The nearest magistrate's court to Braintree is now at Dunmow, a town one sixth of the size of Braintree, and the two places are ten miles apart. It could be argued that your Braintree magistrate hearing a Dunmow case in Dunmow has no more local knowledge than you have.

Whilst the judge need not live in the locality, he should know the place inside and out, from top to bottom, not just from making a ceremonial visit on high days and holidays to the local church—followed by sweet sherry and potato crisps in the mayor's parlour.

And how does he do this? Firstly, his patch must be defined. Easier said than done. Last week a helpful local librarian was unable to define the boundaries of Chiswick. It depended on whether you wanted historical boundaries, electoral boundaries, the licensing boundaries and so on. A large general map is the answer. Secondly, he should always get the local papers, and any local press releases. Thirdly, all judges should meet and mingle together. At some county courts, the judges and district judges lunch together, sometimes with the chief clerk. At the Crown Court the magistrates attend on appeals. Much more needs to be done. At least once a month, the chief probation officer, the prison governor and chief police officer, the local head of the Crown Prosecution Service, counsel, both prosecuting and defending and local solicitors should attend. As it is, we mostly only meet socially at retirement or Christmas parties. The ice melts a little but is seldom broken.

Fourthly, not unlike the new probation boards, there should be a committee of local leaders who meet periodically, both formally and informally, to discuss local issues. The committee should include the local dignitaries, such as the mayor, the police, the magistrates, the probation officers and the local councillors. Local schools, press, churches and businessmen should also be involved. Community leaders representing ethnic interests should be included as a matter of course. If the area has one predominant employer, then have the factory manager or owner. We should also include those local stalwarts who, lacking any official rank, probably do more to hold the community together than many a bureaucrat. The judge should be actively involved, an equal, but not always chairman. The idea that judges are infallible has been undermined over recent years. We now command much less respect than hitherto, so let us face this realistically and work alongside others to achieve justice.

Finally, the judge should get to know the locality by visits made in and out of court hours. Day centres, rehabilitation centres and prisons are obvious places for this but there are many other possibilities, such as schools and hostels. These meetings should be informal and down to earth. The judge should know what happens inside a police station, a probation office, a victim support unit or prison. As it is—when a judge does make such a visit—it is very hard to get a true feel of the place. Clearly security is important, but it has taken somebody of the courage of His Honour Judge Stephen Tumim, H M Inspector of Prisons, really to penetrate the system and to come up with fresh thinking. In short, our training should be radically extended, building on the solid foundation estabished by the Judicial Studies Board.

Judges should have paid sabbaticals to pursue some area of interest connected with their work. Circuit judges are now often appointed in their forties and it is depressing to see some of them ossify with the prospect of their being a judge, uninterrupted, sitting on the bench for over 27 years—not good for them or the public.

A few years ago, I wished to take a month working with NACRO (the National Association for the Care and Resettlement of Offenders) whose leader, Vivien Stern, was keen to have me. My limited efforts to get release met with cold water. This should not be.

Local judges and local sentencing

Too much inconsistency between courts is undesirable—so that there is not really that much scope for local sentencing, despite the Magistrates' Association guidelines which do admit the possibility of local judgments being made. If the same man has stolen some whisky in Kensington and Kennington, fines of £100 and £10 would not be justifiable, but some variation tailored to the specific circumstances should be. Every individual ought to be treated individually. His or her family responsibilities are relevant. Mr Brown the bachelor may welcome Christmas in prison but his co-defendant Mr Black, with wife and small children, would find it intolerable. So would they. It might well destroy that family.

Moreover, although Parliament and the Court of Appeal are entitled to lay down guidelines, let it be roundly said that government is often too concerned with votes—and the civil service too concerned with the Treasury—when it comes to sentencing considerations. The Court of Appeal tinkers with sentences too much. Some of its members are expert criminal lawyers. Some are obviously not. Is it really sensible for them to pontificate over and interfere with decisions reached by experienced criminal judges? The answer must be 'no'.

Local sentencing would have limited application to very serious criminals who cannot expect to avoid imprisonment—and quite rightly so. We are concerned with the middle range of criminals.

As to keeping people out of the criminal system altogether, the local committee should make recommendations which would have to be considered seriously by the relevant authorities. Although the Crown Prosecution Service should be consulted, they are not always right. Neither should they take an entrenched position on a specific offence, regardless of the particular offender involved. When the judge and barristers have reached a sensible agreement on a case, it is frustrating to find it vetoed by the CPS. On occasions, a judge, knowing the views of his local committee, could be asked whether somebody should be prosecuted at all. Cautioning has advantages. Some people should be handled outside the court system altogether. With divorce cases, once the parties have gone to law and the divorce machinery has been set rolling, it is almost impossible to stop. Likewise, with criminal proceedings, it is always harder once the summons has been issued or the indictment has been signed.

Turning to those cases which reach court, most criminals are very inadequate. Of course, they are criminals and should be punished but, day in and day out people come to court partly because of their own inadequacy, often after the most wretched start in life. Violence in the family, sexual abuse, separation of parents (if they had a relationship with their father at all), frequent changes of home, very little money and an inability to handle what money there is—the list is endless. I repeat, these people have committed criminal offences but, whatever the press and the public may say, they should be helped as well as punished. Probation reports are rightly confidential but, suitably edited, some should be made available so that the public can see the other side of the coin. In special hospitals such as Broadmoor, time and time again, the savage rapist or murderer who has shocked yet delighted the public turns out to be most pathetic. The judge has to strike the difficult balance between his duty to the public and the prisoner. It is an art, not a science.

The justification for local justice surely lies in this—that only by breaking justice down into manageable units can it work effectively, for the defendant, the victim and the community. It implies closeness to the community and responsibility to the community. At the present time, although the judge may be attacked by the press and successfully overturned in the Court of Appeal, he is not effectively responsible to the community. Likewise, the defendant, once sentenced, is forgotten, becoming a mere statistic whilst the unfortunate victim hardly figures at all. Only by dealing with matters locally will any sense of mutual responsibility be restored.

The following points may have some attraction. There is no space for detailed consideration.

(a) Justices should sit with judges on sentence. They need not be present throughout the trial although this would help. If they were not, the prosecution should outline the facts and they would then hear the mitigation and read all the reports. Mental Health Review Tribunals consist of a lay person, a pyschiatrist and a judge as president. They often have to make very difficult decisions and, undoubtedly, three minds are better than one as I have found over the last five years as a president.

(b) Plea bargaining should be allowed, usually with the defendant present. Some defendants might plead guilty to avoid imprisonment but it is questionable how many. It is surely more honest for the judge openly to state that if the defendant pleads guilty, thereby showing that he or she is sorry and saving the victim distress, the defendant will not go to prison— but that, on the present facts, if the defendant fights the case, he or she well may. The truth is that judges think like that so why on Earth not say so openly?

(c) The victim's present state of health and views on sentence should be ascertained. He or she should be encouraged to come to court, and should be more involved and more consulted. It is the victim's case: the state has merely taken it over. If practicable, the victim should be paid compensation by the defendant before sentence. Compensation orders are often hard to enforce and the victim's wounds fester for even longer. The victim should *always* be informed of the result of the case and in writing.

(d) The jury know a good deal about the case and no doubt have firm views upon it. Whilst sentence should never be mentioned before they have returned their verdict, once they have done so the jury could be asked to retire again and give their views on sentence—at least a general recommendation. The judge could say, having listened to counsel for both parties, that the possibilities are a fine, supervision or a community service order. What do they think? If prison is inevitable, the judge could say that the range is between one and three years, with half actually being served, what do they think? The judge would explain that he is not bound to follow their views but that he will carefully bear them in mind.

(e) The Probation Service has a difficult task, with a duty to the court and a duty to the defendant. The service has insufficient funds—and too many people to supervise. Voluntary members of the public, looking after no more than six people at any one time could help. They would have to be closely vetted and be

90

trained but, without doubt, their common sense and general experience of life would be extremely valuable. Every community has people of goodwill and good sense with time on their hands. Having read the pre-sentence report the judge could pick a suitable 'defendant's friend'. A young man or young woman with a drink problem might be assigned a middle-aged person, a discreet member of Alcoholics Anonymous, who had almost wrecked his or her own life through drink many years before. These men and women of goodwill exist; let us find them and use them.

(f) Community service orders should be widely used and the judges should be far more actively involved in what the defendants actually do. There are many local claims which need to be met and, within the range of what is available, the judge should decide and the local community should contribute their ideas. There will have to be a filtering system and there may be mistakes made but it is worth investigating.

(g) If the defendant is sent to prison, this prison must be within a reasonable distance of his home and preferably accessible by public transport. At all times, friends and family should know where the prisoner is and, subject to means, they should be assisted in seeing him or her at regular intervals. Local people should be involved in local prisons, helping both staff and inmates If they were more involved there would be less people in them.

Many years ago, I met an old woman at Ryde pier head on the Isle of Wight. She was over seventy, fat and lame with an ulcerated leg. Her son was in Parkhurst prison. His wife and children had severed contact and his mother was his only friend. She lived in East London and with considerable difficulty and courage visited her son once a month. Drinking tea, waiting for the Portsmouth ferry, I found it hard to contain my admiration for her and my contempt for the system which so unjustly punished her and her son. Whatever the difficulties, he should have been in a London prison.

Two final points. Firstly, local courts should be more open and user-friendly. They should have open days. Specific cases should never be discussed, but judges and staff should be available for questions. Even educated people find the court system daunting. We must dispel this impression. I make visitors welcome even though some of the questions afterwards are not easy to answer.

Secondly, backed by the local committee, the court should be able to make suggestions which carry weight and authority. The longer a case the more we all get to know the background and, repeatedly, ideas come to mind as to how to avoid the same thing happening again. For instance, that pedestrian crossing is wrongly sited. That public house is badly laid out with a weak publican and inadequate bouncers. That underpass, close to the cinema, is badly lit and obscured by bushes. That garage forecourt should be covered by a video camera.

All concerned in the case, victim, witnesses, jury or judge, even defendant should be able to make suggestions, knowing that these suggestions will be properly and speedily considered—and monitored by the press. Likewise, if someone deserves to be publicly thanked and rewarded, small sums should be available and this should be done openly in court. At the moment, when a judge makes a suggestion it is always politely acknowledged but does it ever really go much further than that?

For Chiswick, read Acton or Royston or Norwich or Bracknell or Aldeburgh or Oxford—or wherever you live. The essential point is local courts with local judges for local communities.

Postscript

These views are personal and not official—but official views are only personal views stamped official. Like the curate's egg, I hope they are found 'good in parts'.

Note

1 HMSO, *A New Framework for Local Justice,* Cm 1829 (London: HMSO, 1992).

CHAPTER 7

Justice in the Community: The New Zealand Experience

Fred McElrea

At the heart of the usual Western concept of criminal justice is the idea of a contest between the state and the accused, conducted according to well defined rules of fair play and leading to a verdict, guilty or not guilty. One of the most important of these rules is the presumption of innocence—the accused is to be found 'not guilty' unless the state can prove otherwise. Those found guilty are punished by the state, and of course the more punitive the sentencing regime the greater is the incentive for a guilty person to rely on the presumption of innocence and put the state to the proof, ie not to plead guilty.

What do these elementary propositions have to do with Relational Justice? They have a great deal to do with relationships, and, I suggest, a considerable influence on our system of criminal justice. Let me explain.

The concept of a fair trial has been described as the apotheosis of the adversary system—its highest ideal. It has come to be seen in procedural terms, formulated by complex rules of evidence (eg the exclusion of hearsay evidence), the Judges' rules for the conduct of police interviews, and other settled principles of 'due process'. Important though these are in themselves, they tend to have pre-occupied our thinking in criminal justice. The over-riding issue is whether fair *procedures* are followed—not whether they produce a just result, a fair outcome for the accused, satisfaction for the victim or harmony in the community to which both victim and offender belong. We seem to be stuck in a mould, formed mostly in the nineteenth century, which measures justice by its own procedures. Indeed much of the language used is from that era. Following the taking of 'depositions' the accused is 'arraigned' upon an 'indictment'. The accused stands in 'the dock', almost like an exhibit on display. 'You are charged that on or about . . . you did . . . How do you plead?' The whole trial is conducted very publicly, with accompanying rituals that serve to dramatise and hence to de-personalise the experience.

It is perhaps not surprising that the news media increasingly treat crime as prime news, and criminal trials as free drama or live entertainment, sometimes not very far advanced from gladiatorial combat. They thrive on conflict, on public contests, on finding winners and losers. If the victim features at all it is usually as a 'loser', even where the accused has also 'lost', so the only 'winner' is the prosecution, that is, the impersonal state. Feelings of antagonism, fear, anger and general negativity are fuelled, amongst the trial participants and the viewing public alike. There is scarcely ever any good news from the courts. Crime rates seem to keep climbing and prison populations keep growing, at considerable expense in human and financial terms. The needs of neither offenders nor victims are satisfied. The existing theoretical bases of punishment seem bankrupt and in the world of criminal justice morale is fairly low.

But there is another way of doing justice, one which can promote the acceptance of responsibility and by a consensual process seek to heal the wounds caused by crime. It is already at work in the youth court in New Zealand, so it is not just an idealistic sentiment. It has the potential to transform adult courts as well.

The youth court model at work
Under the Children Young Persons and Their Families Act 1989 offending by 'young persons'—ie young people of at least 14 years of age but under 17—is the jurisdiction of a specialist youth court. Potentially this court can deal with all offences except murder and manslaughter, although very serious offences such as rape are usually referred on to the adult courts. In deciding whether a disputed charge is proved the adversary system is maintained in full (with one exception, concerning pleading, which I mention later). However, in disposing of admitted or proved offences a radically new system is in force. The key component is the Family Group Conference (FGC), convened and facilitated by a youth justice co-ordinator, a Department of Social Welfare employee.

The FGC is attended by the young person, members of his family (including his extended family), the victim (often accompanied by supporters), a youth advocate (if requested by the young person), a police officer (usually a member of the specialist *Youth Aid* division), a social worker (in certain cases only), and anyone else that members of the family wish to be there. This last category might include a representative of a community organisation, drug addiction agency or community work sponsor seen as potentially helpful to the young person. There is no limit on the number of persons who can attend an FGC. The usual range is probably around six to 12 persons, but occasionally one hears of 20 or more people attending. Judges do not attend FGCs. To do so would disempower others present. It is up to the youth justice co-ordinator to chair the meeting in such a way as to enable feelings to be expressed and all points of view to be heard. Victims may need to be encouraged to bring supporters so that they do not feel overwhelmed by a solid turn-out of the offender's family, something that has attracted criticism in the past. Any decision of the FGC requires the agreement of all present, including the young person, the victim and the police representative. This should mean that a less powerful voice is not over-ridden, and it also has the result that where the conference is not unanimous the matter is decided by the court.

Matters can reach an FGC by one of two routes. The 1989 Act has a strong diversionary emphasis to it, and without invoking the jurisdiction of the court at all the police can refer an admitted offence to an FGC. If the members of the FGC all agree, including the police officer present, the matter is handled as decided by the FGC and will not go to court. Over 80 per cent of matters are handled in this way. Secondly, all offences admitted or proved in the youth court must be referred to an FGC, which recommends to the court how the matter should be dealt with. Occasionally an FGC recommends a sanction to be imposed by the court. Usually it puts forward a plan of action, eg apology, reparation (in money or work for the victim), community work, a curfew and/or an undertaking to attend school or not to associate with co-offenders. The court is usually asked to adjourn proceedings, say for three to four months, to allow the plan to be implemented and the proceedings to be withdrawn. The youth court nearly always accepts such plans, recognising that the scheme of the Act places the primary power of disposition with the FGC. However, in serious cases the court can use a wide range of court-imposed sanctions.

The human dynamics involved in an FGC depend (and build) on the relationships between all those present, but the importance of the presence of the victim is repeatedly stressed.

> The crux of the Youth Justice system is *direct* involvement of the offender and the 'offended against', eyeball-to-eyeball . . . When victims and families farewell each other with smiles, handshakes and embraces, I know that justice has been served.[1]

> The FGC exposes young offenders to the most devastating responsibility of seeing and hearing the consequences of their actions when a victim is present.[2]

> The primary objectives of a criminal justice system must include healing the breach of social harmony, of social relationships, putting right the wrong and making reparation rather than concentrating on punishment. The ability of the victim to have input at the family group conference is, or ought to be, one of the most significant virtues of the youth justice procedures. On the basis of

our experience to date, we can expect to be amazed at the generosity of spirit of many victims and (to the surprise of many professionals participating) the absence of retributive demands and vindictiveness. Victims' responses are in direct contrast to the hysterical, media-generated responses to which we are so often exposed.[3]

In the courtroom itself the judge's role is very different. I make a point of welcoming the family and thanking them for being there. I also encourage them to speak—by asking them to tell me how they found the FGC procedure, for example. I try to involve the young person, perhaps by asking him to explain to me the main parts of the FGC plan. So the participation of others is welcomed. In addition to legal representation there will often be a family spokesperson who will talk to the judge—often a very powerful spokesperson. Overall, the concept of a judge trying to facilitate the strengths of others and bring them to the fore is radically different to the controlling position of the traditional judge.

Responsible reconciliation

The distinctive elements of this youth court model are threefold:

(a) the transfer of power from the state, principally the Courts' power, to the community;

(b) the Family Group Conference as a mechanism for producing a negotiated, community response;

(c) the involvement of victims as key participants, making possible a healing process for both offender and victim.

Taken together these elements have produced an approach to justice which is centred around right relationships. The prevailing spirit I would characterize as *responsible reconciliation*. The term 'reconciliation' connotes a positive, growing process where strength is derived from the interaction of victim, offender and family in a supportive environment. It is a 'responsible' process in that those most directly affected take responsibility for what has happened, and for what is to happen. Indeed it is an environment in which co-responsibility can be fostered, recognising that fault does not usually lie entirely with the offender and encouraging others who share that responsibility to shoulder it. It can be a moving experience to hear from a grandmother who has been working closely with a wayward grandson and in the process has let her own son know how he has let the youngster down.

It is natural that the emphasis should be on families when dealing with young people, because families are their natural community, the source of their relationships, of dependence or interdependence, and the most likely basis of social control. However the influence of families upon their members (and vice versa) does not cease at a given age, say the seventeenth birthday. As they grow up, young people are likely to continue to depend upon family in varying degrees to meet some of their emotional and social needs.

One common criticism of the more traditional and 'antiseptic' model of justice is that it has largely removed the element of shame. In the youth court model, shame can be experienced in a creative and constructive way. This is because the young person is dealt with in the context of his or her family relationships and not in isolation. For a lot of families their young people's offending is a matter of shame, and if that shame is experienced by family members with the youngster at the conference, he cannot just shrug it off. I remember reading of one young man explaining that it was easy to be 'staunch' or 'cool' in court (and indeed to take some pride in being there) but at a family group conference, he explained, *'You're just a flea, man — you're nothing!'*

Only in the context of relationships meaningful to the offender can there be effective shaming and a change of attitude. We may think that the traditional court system holds offenders accountable but it has become too de-personalised to succeed in many cases. As the Austrian criminologist Christa Pelikan has pointed out[4], mediation processes have an empathetic and educative effect by way of an *'inner drama'* which has a socialising value for juveniles. By contrast, she says, the *'outer drama'* seen in the courtroom too often produces the opposite effect—an inner withdrawal, the operation of defence mechanisms, a shunning of the deep-rooted acceptance of responsibility. Similarly the Australian criminologist John Braithwaite[5] distinguishes between 'stigmatising shame' which excludes, isolates and degrades, and 're-integrative shame' which accepts the offender, offers a new beginning and can be a powerful agent for change. These distinctions are found at work in the youth court model.

I have mentioned that the adversary method of pleading is not followed in the youth court. I now see this as an important difference in principle. On first appearing in court the young person may volunteer that the charge is denied—in which case it is adjourned for a hearing—but otherwise no plea is taken and the matter is adjourned for an FGC to be held. There the prosecution summary of the relevant facts is discussed and the young person can admit or deny its contents. This is done in the presence of the victim so that there is an opportunity to try and reach agreement on the facts.

What is significant in this process is that the acceptance of responsibility is done not within the ritual of plea taking in court, but at the FGC in the presence of the young offender's lawyer, family, the victim, and other community representatives. Furthermore this change of emphasis is reinforced by the principle expounded in the statute[6] that young people committing offences should be 'held accountable, and encouraged to accept responsibility, for their behaviour' and should be 'dealt with in a way that acknowledges their needs and that will give them the opportunity to develop in responsible, beneficial and socially acceptable ways'. These provisions emphasise accountability and membership of a wider community.

Origins and scope

It is important for outside observers to realise that on a comparative basis, and despite its 'pacific' setting, New Zealand is reported to have high rates of offending, of victimisation and of incarceration[7]. Any success of the youth court model has not been achieved in a low-crime culture. Nevertheless the new system did not grow out of such considerations, and nor was it adopted by reading the latest criminological studies or studying the latest overseas experiments in mediation. Michael Doolan[8] outlines the concerns and the process that led to the Children Young Persons and Their Families Act 1989. It is significant that the New Zealand Parliament's Select Committee from February to April 1988 travelled to Maori and Pacific Island meeting places throughout hearing submissions on how to recast the Bill so as to make it more culturally relevant to Polynesian people, as well as simpler and less bureaucratic in its operation. I believe the FGC mechanism which was the result of that process is the direct descendant of the 'whanau conference' long employed by Maori people, although it is adapted to suit its new context, eg by inclusion of the police.

> It is not suggested that the old Maori ways should now be restored, but that ought not inhibit the search for a greater sense of family and community involvement and responsibility in the maintenance of law and order. At present there is little room for a community input into individual sentencing, no chance for an offender's family to express censure or support, no opportunity for a reconciliation between the wrongdoer and the aggrieved, no search for a community solution to a social problem. The right and responsibility of a community to care for its own is again taken away and shifted to the comparatively anonymous institutions of Western law.[9]

When the legislators adopted and adapted the model of a whanau conference, other aspects inherent in this community-based model were bound to accompany it. I rather suspect that non-Polynesian eyes simply failed to see the significance of what was being offered. But it would be a huge mistake to see the benefits of the new model as there primarily for

Polynesian peoples. Like other industrialised countries, New Zealand is a multi-cultural society and the youth court serves equally the rich and the poor, urban and rural communities, and all races and creeds. Indeed one of its strengths has been identified as its ability to reach across such boundaries and help build better relationships within and between communities.

New possibilities

But what of the relationships of adult offenders? Would they be amenable to the notion of a family-based conference? I suggest that families are still likely to play an important role for most adults. Naturally family ties will change in character as young people mature. There may be less dependence or discipline, and more friendship and respect. As some family ties become less meaningful or are lost entirely, eg through death, divorce or abuse, others may take their place when the individual marries, has children, and so on.

In any event we must look to the wider web of relationships and ask whether there are other relationships of respect, other communities to which the offender belongs. If so, these might be a substitute for, or a valuable supplement to, family relationships. Tony Marshall argues that in our mobile society, the concept of community can embrace meaningful associations on many bases—'work, school, voluntary associations based on leisure pursuits, political parties, churches . . . ethnic groups, trades unions, extended family, etc.'[10] Our needs for acceptance, self-affirmation, social involvement, friendship, fun, and spiritual sustenance do not evaporate with adulthood or 'independence'; they all require that we sustain meaningful relationships with others.

This leads me to the notion of a Community Group Conference (CGC)—an adult equivalent of an FGC which would seek to tap the relationships of respect and influence that apply to the adult offender. Are there family members who are or might become concerned for his or her well-being? Is there an employer, work-mate, fellow football player, former teacher or school friend who still can provide meaning and support? A small group of such people could be invited to the conference, along with the victim and supporters and a police representative. Very few people can be quite without any family or other meaningful relationships and it would be wrong to shape a model of justice around them. It may be a question of starting with whatever relational matrix the offender has and building a CGC around that. Where there is difficulty in assembling a community group there may be a place for voluntary associations (a local church group, cultural association, or service organisation) to step into the gap.

The importance of an FGC is that it brings together several representatives of the community to which a young person relates so as to provide a negotiated, community response. The task in respect of adults is, I suggest, exactly the same. The object is to get the relevant community to take responsibility for helping the offender to address the wrong he has done, repair the damage, and to affirm him in any remedial steps for the future. In the process the victim's needs are addressed, and the offender can be restored to a place of respect in the community.

Since first raising the possibility of a CGC process for adults I have heard of at least two such conferences successfully arranged on a voluntary basis, in each case with very positive results for both victim and offender. And such statistics as there are from the youth court suggest that the number of cases in court[11] and the proportion of those where the court would be required to impose sentence would both be likely to drop substantially under a system of CGCs for adults. The proportion of custodial sentences is also likely to drop sharply, if the youth court experience[12] is relevant. FGCs strive to find community-based solutions and often produce a more imaginative and suitable plan than the courts could achieve. Where an FGC has recommended something other than prison, the knowledge that the victim has agreed to that plan has a palpable effect on the judge. Gone is the assumption that the state represents the victim in seeking a punitive sanction.

New responsibilities

In the New Zealand family court there has long been an obligation on lawyers to promote reconciliation. In various civil jurisdictions there is starting to appear an obligation to consider alternative dispute resolution procedures.[13] Why could not a new Criminal Justice Act impose a responsibility on lawyers to encourage offenders towards reconciliation with victims, and to start that process by admitting their responsibility (if any) for the harm done? This has little appeal under the present system, but as part of a new deal for victims and offenders it would be a different proposition. When the consequences of admitting guilt are rejection and isolation, and imprisonment holds out only the prospect of degradation and destruction of self-respect, there is little reason to plead guilty. But if that is changed into a positive, growing and healing experience, if the consequences are intended to promote reconciliation, there is an incentive to accept responsibility.

Howard Zehr criticises the adversary system for encouraging denials of responsibility:

Even if he is legally guilty, his attorney will likely tell him to plead 'not guilty' at some stage. In legal terms 'not guilty' is the way one says 'I want a trial' or 'I need more time'. All of this tends to obscure the experiential and moral reality of guilt and innocence.[14]

In the past the law has concentrated on the dangers of convicting one innocent person and has so arranged the laws of evidence and procedure that this risk is reduced to a minimum—even if (so it was said) 100 guilty people go free. When a person could be hanged for stealing, that was understandable, but now it is perhaps time to acknowledge *each* wrong trial result as an injustice. Is it not time to stop and ask: What does it do to the person who is *in fact* guilty to be found 'not guilty'? And when that happens what does it do also to the victim, to victim-offender (and other) relationships, and to the respect for justice in the community?

I am not suggesting that the adversary model be dropped, or that the presumption of innocence be abandoned, but it should not be assumed that there are no personal or social costs incurred when the guilty are declared 'not guilty'. I am sure the wider society would support a system that encouraged those who are guilty to admit their guilt and focus their attention on putting right the wrong they have done. The legal process, even for defendants who plead guilty, fails to confront offenders with the reality of their offending. Unlike the young person at an FGC, the adult offender does not experience on the one hand the hurt and anger of the victim, nor on the other hand the understanding, forgiveness and even support that can follow a genuine and personal expression of contrition. And any feelings of victimisation on the offender's part are likely to be accentuated by punishment handed down in the name of a faceless state.

Conclusion

What is the prospect of public acceptance of such a model of criminal justice?

Properly explained, I believe it is good, and this for a host of reasons. It is not a soft system. Facing a victim is commonly said to be far harder than facing a court. FGC plans are often both tougher and more imaginative than court-imposed sentences. An acceptance of responsibility for one's own actions is an ideal that few would oppose. The strengthening of family and community-based relationships could not be politically unpopular. A much better deal for victims is what the public has long sought. A lesser role for the state and a greater role for local communities is consistent with reforms underway in many Western countries. There is also the prospect of fiscal savings from the reduced use of courts and prisons, although offset against this must be the cost of putting more resources into the community. The idea of negotiated justice is either accepted or gaining ground in other contexts, such as the use of mediation in family courts and in civil litigation. And finally, there is ample evidence that the public is not as vengeful as some politicians seem to think.

It would hardly have been thinkable under the old system for a young man to be motivated to write to his elderly victim the letter I recently saw.

> . . . I wish I could turn back the hand of time and go back to that day and help you with your bag to the top of the hill instead of snatching it from your hands. I would have had the chance to know you and talk to you. I am so sorry for hurting you.

I believe we can design a system that repairs relationships and teaches respect where there was none before. When that happens we will truly have a system of justice—not a sterile, rule-bound creature but one that breathes the spirit of justice.

Notes

[1] T Stewart, *The Youth Court in New Zealand; a New Model of Justice*, (Auckland: Legal Research Foundation, 1993) A Youth Justice Co-ordinator who has co-ordinated several hundred conferences, from her article in at pp 43,49.

[2] R Clark, (August/September 1993) Auckland, Victim Support, in *Te Rangatahi* [Youth Justice newsletter] #1, p 4.

[3] Principal Youth Court Judge MJA Brown (25 September - 1 October 1993) in *Listener*, p 7, 'Viewpoint'.

[4] *Who wants what kind of justice?* a paper written for the 11th International Criminology Congress, Budapest, August 1993.

[5] J Braithwaite, *Crime, Shame and Reintegration* (Cambridge: CUP, 1989).

[6] Section 4(f) Children, Young Persons and Their Families Act, 1989.

[7] New Zealand is second only to the USA in the rate of imprisonment of its population.

[8] Legal Research Foundation publication (above), pp 19-21.

[9] *PUAO-TE-ATA-TU* (Day break), the report of the Ministerial Advisory Committee on a Maori perspective for the Department of Social Welfare, September 1988, p 74.

[10] T Marshall, *Criminal Justice in the New Community* (York: paper written for the British Criminology Conference, 1991), p 13.

[11] G M Maxwell, and A Morris, in *Commonwealth Judicial Journal*, Vol 9 No 4 (1992), p 26. 'Only 16 per 1,000 young people appeared in the youth court in 1990 [the first complete year] compared with an average of 63 per 1,000 in the three calendar years immediately preceding the Act'.

[12] The number of children admitted to Social Welfare Department residences dropped from 2,712 in 1988 to 923 in 1992-93.

13 'The obligation of our profession is, or has long been thought to be, to serve as healers of human conflict. To fulfil our traditional obligation means that we should provide mechanisms that can produce an acceptable result in the shortest possible time, with the least possible expense, and with a minimum of stress on the participants ... That is what justice is all about.'—Warren Burger, former Chief Justice, US Supreme Court.

14 H Zehr, *Changing Lenses — A New Focus for Crime and Justice* (Herald Press,1990), p 67.

CHAPTER 8

Youth Crime: A Relational Perspective

John Harding

Who are the young people who commit crime? What kind of backgrounds do they come from? What can be done by professionals and ordinary members of the community to help a young offender to break free from crime into responsible adulthood?

We start with the assumption that the commission of crime by young people is not uncommon. One in three young men under the age of 30 will have been cautioned by the police or found guilty by a court. The peak age for male offending is 18 and the peak age for female offending is 15. Fortunately, most offending by young people is relatively minor, involving theft of property or criminal damage. Less than two out of ten young people who are cautioned return to the attention of the police within two years. Delinquency is thus treated as a passing phase once the normal processes of adolescent development have been allowed to occur through the school, the family and local community links.

For some young people, however, offending is more problematic in that their offences are serious or persistent or—in rare cases—a combination of both. Even here, the tradition over the past decade has been for probation officers and social workers working in close co-operation with the police and members of a young person's family to develop highly individualised ways of addressing the behaviour of a persistent young offender, in tandem with looking at the offender's other social needs. Every effort is made to hold on to troublesome young people within the family and the neighbourhood in the knowledge that residential placements—be they young offender institutions or secure accommodation run by local authorities and with all the accompanying stigma of temporary exile, exclusion and alienation from what is normal—have a poor track record in terms of keeping children and young people out of trouble on their return to the community.

Over the past two years, this reasoned orthodoxy—which led to the reduction in the use of custody by the courts for young people under the age of 17 from a high of over 8,000 a year in 1981 to less than 2,000 in 1991—has been questioned and potentially undermined by a harsher rhetoric framed by politicians and the editors of tabloid newspapers. It exhorts us to *condemn* a little more and to *understand* a little less. A week hardly passes in which the public is not treated to the demonic behaviour of some fresh 'Rat boy' (the name given to one young offender by the media), or to overindulgent social workers who have let another allegedly incorrigible youngster spend a vacation at the expense of allegedly angry tax-payers.

At one level, it is right that the government, the public and the press are concerned about persistent offenders. Impulsive or reckless criminality should concern everyone, and it certainly does concern the victims of crime, many of whom live cheek-by-jowl on the run down estates of our towns and cities. However, condemnation and lack of understanding merely lead to stereotypical responses and a search for instant solutions that suggest the offender is somehow qualitatively different from the rest of us. The late Baroness Wootten, a criminologist and an experienced justice of the peace, had a neat way of making the point

> Juvenile courts cater for other people's children but not for their own.

If we have failed at all in recent years it is not in being 'soft on crime' as many detractors would have us believe. Rather, it is in not adequately explaining to the public and the media the nature of our responsibilities, in particular the stories that young people who are in trouble have to tell about their sad, chaotic and blighted lives. Perhaps we should show youngsters' faces, tell their stories, reveal their secrets (including abuse by adults) and lay out the uncomfortable meanings of their lives.

By way of illustration, two narratives, both tragic in the sense that early broken relationships led to further loss and victimisation, come to mind. Not long ago, I received a letter from a life-sentence prisoner serving out his time at HM Prison, Kingston. The man, in his mid-forties, catalogued the impact of residential care in children's homes and prison confinement over a period of 30 years. The narrative in his letter was peppered with a sense of loss and institutionalisation.

> All my life it seems I've been running but all I ever wanted was to belong somewhere and yet I've never found it . . . Deep down, I'm a lonely person and the loneliest place I know is prison, 'cos life is empty and nothing ever changes . . . one day!

Shortly after this written encounter, I met a man at a youth crime conference. His son, aged 18, had been brutally and tragically murdered in Reading in a manner which replicated a scene from a cult horror film. The murderer, according to the victim's father, had drifted from divorcing parents to school truancy, to casual shack-ups, to a complete retreat from reality. The sense of alienation and reckless self-regard reminded me of the first murderer in Shakespeare's *Macbeth*.

> I am one, my Liege, whom the vile blows and buffets of the world hath so incensed that I am reckless what I do to spite the world.

The victim's father felt that the only way he could make some sense of his son's untimely death was to devote himself to part-time youth work, to create opportunities for young people wherever possible. He was forcibly reminded of the need of the public—as well as that of the caring and controlling services—to pay attention, in detail, to those young people in despair who can make little sense of their lives.

Understanding delinquency

In seeking to understand young offenders, there is a prevailing tendency to characterize them as a rapidly multiplying, homogeneous group Research tells a quite different story. Several groups of young offenders emerge, each with different needs, requirements and prognoses. Spencer Millham, the Professor in charge of the Dartington Social Research Unit, using a cohort of research studies, has identified five different criminal careers among young people.[1]

Temporary delinquents

Firstly, there are temporary delinquents. This accurately describes the vast majority of young offenders, who usually commit crime in the company of others. Their crimes are of a minor nature and the rewards, emotional as well as financial, are too small to encourage the transient delinquent to repeat the experiment. They are usually diverted from crime by way of a police caution and most are unlikely to repeat their offending behaviour.

Difficult and disturbed young people

The second group of young offenders can be characterized as difficult and disturbed. Such young people also have a temporary involvement in crime but their offending is linked to wider problems such as conflict within the home or difficulties in the classroom. With specialist attention by education remedial services, combined with the supportive supervision of probation or social services, such youngsters can improve and thrive.

Persistent offenders

The third group, representing the motive force behind the introduction by government of secure training centres in the Criminal Justice and Public Order Act 1994, are persistent offenders. Very quickly, the persistent delinquent accumulates three or maybe more criminal convictions and a custodial placement threatens. In one of the best known studies of delinquent boys, tracked over a period of twenty years, West and Farrington describe their subjects as having the following characteristics:[2]

- They are from low income families.
- They are from large families with a criminal parent.
- They are from families which exercise poor supervision of their children
- They were often of low intelligence and troublesome at school.

More recently, at the request of the Home Office, the Policy Studies Institute carried out a survey of 533 persistent young offenders between the ages of ten to sixteen.[3] Analysis of the interviews with 74 of these re-offenders indicates that the majority had left school, and many had nothing to do with their free time, not being employed, training or studying. A high proportion of the girls in the sample were pregnant or had a child. School had been a negative experience and many of the young people had been excluded from schools, only to leave the educational system permanently.

The interviews and social services data confirmed a picture of severe familial disruption and 'relational' dysfunction. Half of the sample were known to their social services departments and the original contact with that department was more likely to have been for welfare than criminal reasons. The researchers stated that these persistent offenders gave the impression of a mixture of chaos, sadness and boredom. Their aspirations for the future were normal in the sense of wanting to settle down, have a family and find work. The actuality was less rosy.

'One-off' serious offenders

The remaining two groups of young offenders were very different. First there is the one-off serious offender whose crimes are rare and isolated, such as the two assailants of the infant Jamie Bulger. The offence appears to come out of the blue and is not necessarily explained by social factors. Such offenders will be 'detained under section 53' (ie long term detention under section 53 Children and Young Persons Act 1933) usually in a youth treatment centre. For these youngsters detention in secure settings involving psycho-therapeutic or behaviour modifying treatment is generally effective, especially if it focuses on the family situation. However, if the home situation is unstable, it is vital that social services are also involved to support the troubled family, preparing them for the eventual return of the serious offender.

Persistent and serious offenders

Finally, there is the persistent and serious offender who represents a combination of the children in the preceding two groups. Research indicates that the prospects are bleak for such offenders, for even if the problems that led to the serious offences are successfully treated, subsequent reconviction for a property offence remains a likely prospect.

Responding to crime—A multi-dimensional strategy

The preceding pages show that crime is a complex phenomenon, in which understanding and careful intelligence gathering are crucial elements. Better information is needed to assess the number and characteristics of young offenders, the nature, scale and frequency of their offending and the patterns of their criminal careers including responses to new experiences and opportunities as well as action by the police and courts. Systematic information is also needed about the nature, cost and effectiveness of programmes to prevent and reduce crime and criminality; about the cost and suffering caused by offences committed by young people, and about the nature, cost and effectiveness of the procedures for dealing with youth crime through the criminal justice process.

Responding to crime is not the responsibility of a single agency or any number of public officials. The vast majority of crime goes undetected. Only three in every hundred offences leads to a subsequent conviction and sentence. Thus the criminal justice process itself is a narrow and blunt instrument for dealing with the causes of crime and its prevention. Crime prevention measures, particularly where targeted on areas of a connurbation where there are multiple forms of social and economic deprivation, are likely to have a number of beneficial effects. This is always provided that sponsoring bodies—be they local authorities or public protection agencies—work in partnership, focus on matters together, and collaborate with local citizens and families so that they are empowered to bring about change for themselves.

What kind of crime prevention programmes are most likely to reduce the likelihood of crime whilst strengthening the capacity of children and families to function more effectively? The Relational Justice theme highlights dysfunctional human inter-relationships as both a significant contributory cause of crime and thus as an important focus for any prevention strategy. At a seminar organised by Action on Youth Crime, a multi-disciplinary gathering of practitioners and policy makers found no difficulty whatsoever in identifying strategies that had the capacity to make a difference to people's lives. They included an expansion of nursery education, family centres to provide support and practical help to isolated parents or to families under stress: for the schoolchild, combatting exclusion from school and ensuring alternative provision when exclusion has, in the last resort, to take place nonetheless; for young people, making sure that the local youth service has an outreach programme that attracts the most marginalised youngsters and makes links with other forms of voluntary and statutory provision. Here, with the decline in the unskilled job market and the fact that 16 and 17-year-olds are presently ineligible for income support it is vital that the young are given support and access to training and employment schemes. It is important also to provide 'safe houses'—places of asylum—for young people who can no longer cope with abuse or unresolved conflict within their own family.

The scarcity of funding for existing preventative work and initiatives contrasts sharply with the amount of money that is readily made available for new correctional institutions such as secure training centres, where the total cost per child is likely to exceed £2,000 a week. Evidence from the USA suggests that a dollar invested in preventative work with children and families will in time save seven dollars which would otherwise have been spent on various forms of adult incarceration and the associated costs of the criminal justice process.

The scope of criminal justice

The youth courts—introduced under the Criminal Justice Act 1991—have an extensive range of sentencing dispositions ranging from dicharges, fines and community based penalties to custody for young people under 18 (75 per cent of whom will be 16 or 17 year old males). Before a sentence is passed it is important that a probation officer or social worker prepares a pre-sentence report that addresses offending behaviour, family background and social circumstances, and localises a plan of action that is likely to gain the commitment of the young person and his or her family. Such plans must carry weight and influence with magistrates and judges.

How do young offenders respond to court imposed penalties? We know from studies on sanctions for serious or persistent young offenders under the age of 20 conducted by Gill McIvor of Stirling University[4] that no single approach or sentence is ever likely to be effective with all offenders in terms of reducing subsequent recidivism.

Community service orders occupy a particularly useful place in the range of intermediate sanctions for young offenders, especially, it seems, if the placement is personalised for the offender who can then see that his or her effort is appreciated by beneficiaries such as pensioners or the disabled. Most offenders on community service in England and Wales complete the sentence satisfactorily—the success rate is 70 per cent. There is also evidence that offenders find community service to be a worthwhile and meaningful experience, without this detracting from the punitive impact of that sanction. A survey in Scotland indicates that the overwhelming majority of individuals who have been in receipt of work undertaken by offenders, and agencies who have offered placements, greatly valued the work carried out.[5] But offenders are unlikely to do well on community service if beset by a range of intractable personal problems and addictive behaviour.

With older youths, groupwork based on the problem solving model—and which is offence focused or which is concerned with the development of personal and social skills—has been shown to be associated with reduced re-offending. Young adults who are on the brink of custody for the commission of relatively serious property offences such as burglary or fraud are frequently required to attend day centre sessions as part of a condition of a probation order.

Offenders who are assessed as having a low likelihood of recidivism will, on the other hand, benefit most from less intrusive measures and may do relatively worse if subject to instructive conditions or they are exposed to the influence of high risk offenders who are more criminally sophisticated.

Family interventions may have some success with juvenile offenders, and approaches which teach parents how to negotiate and monitor behavioural contracts appear to have shown promise. The value of family focused work may lie in the ability of the workers to change both the delinquent's behaviour and his or her immediate family network.[6] However, situations to which young offenders return after involvement in community based programmes can be more important determinants of subsequent success than the programmes themselves. As one American study concluded,[7] attempts should be made to work with delinquent youths in the context of their social networks.

Farrington, in surveying the scope of delinquency prevention in the USA and Britain, lays special emphasis on early intervention in the families of anti-social children. The American 'Head Start' projects—which combine pre-school enrichment programmes with home visits and parental management training—sustained disadvantaged children through adolescence into adulthood with remarkably good results in terms of low offending and scholastic attainment in comparison with a control group.[8]

In a Canadian study, Andrews and his colleagues[9] noted the effectiveness of using trained volunteers from the community with high risk young offenders, especially where there is intensive contact on a one-to-one basis. Offenders who were dealt with by volunteers, reported having made more open and warm relationships with their supervisors and receiving more vital assistance and help than those young offenders supervised by hard pressed professional probation officers. One particular side effect of this research is worth describing. 'Anti-criminal modelling', in which supervisors serve as role models to reinforce good behaviour, was also associated with reduced recidivism among probationers supervised by volunteers but not among those supervised by professional workers, where the lessened contact rendered this approach impractical.

The Hampshire Probation Service partnership with the National Childrens' Home, offers a particularly effective example of this process in relation to young adults aged between 16 and 20 who are placed with paid volunteers from the community in a short-term foster care project. Most of the subjects come from a background of broken families, care placements with local authorities, young offender institutions and they have a record of persistent property offences. The average stay is six months. The young people are offered accommodation and supportive help by the volunteers in an attempt to re-focus their lives and to break loose from the influences which propelled them into crime. Kevin said of his experience with a carer:

> It's an opportunity. Somewhere stable to live. I got into a bit of trouble before. I was living in childrens' homes but now I don't feel I need to go out stealing cars.

A carer commented:

> When I first read about the scheme I thought 'Who in their right mind?' But when I became more involved and understood more about what the scheme was about and the support available I realised that it is an invaluable resource. It gives offenders an opportunity to rebuild their lives in a normal environment which will address their individual needs. If they're prepared to make the commitment then it's probably the best way of dealing with them!

McIvor, in her review of programmes, concludes that there is little evidence that punitive, institutional regimes have much of an impact on recidivism. If the past gives us any indication of the future, the record of approved schools in England and Wales—or, indeed, of the training schools for twelve to 15 year old boys in Northern Ireland—with their questionable educational regimes and high recidivism rates—give little hope that the five planned secure training centres in England will achieve their purpose in reclaiming youngsters from delinquent ways.

The best hope of reducing persistent offending behaviour among the young is to carefully identify which type of approach works best with which type of offender. This perspective suggests that the responsible agencies should always seek to develop a wide range of options for young people which are adequately funded and staffed by committed professionals with a clear sense of purpose and common standards of practice. In recognition of the multiple needs of troubled young people, staff will be required to make broad based coalitions not only with a range of statutory and voluntary agencies (which can provide key services such as accommodation, job finding and further education) but also with the communities that are local to the offender.

Breaking the chain of anti-social behaviour *is* possible. It requires a range of preventative measures in the community, all the way from improved pre-natal care to post-custodial supervision for the older adolescent. Given the link between offending and other social problems, measures that succeed in reducing crime have benefits that go far beyond this. Large scale studies suggest that crime reduction measures will have pay-offs in terms of reduced alcohol abuse, less family violence, less drug abuse, fewer school failures, and reduced truancy and unemployment rates.

In the final analysis, the community should always seek to strengthen and support the ties of family and neighbourhood, no matter how fragile such arrangements may appear on the surface. These links and their preservation are often what matters most to the young in their struggle to make sense of their lives.

Concluding thoughts

Over the past two years, young offenders have become a major political issue—to the point where sweeping generalisations, gross stereotypes and 'quick fix' responses have overshadowed more reasoned discussion, better information and a proper search for what works in reducing offending behaviour. The ensuing panic legislation leads us, inexorably, to the creation of new institutions that will further exclude and alienate the already marginalised young—confirming rather than challenging delinquent identities. Such temporary expulsion of persistent offenders is unlikely, according to the research of the Policy Studies Institute, to reduce the level of crime by more than a small fraction.

Without some local context in which young offenders can relate their offending behaviour to the victims of crime, they can, within isolated institutions, so easily neutralise the impact of what they have done by assuming denial or by minimising the gravity of their behaviour. They may rationalise that the victim was well off and had plenty of insurance cover. They will not be conscious of the fear of crime that they have generated in the mind of the victim or his or her family. Victims, too, can be left in a state of confusion and anger; with many questions unresolved. They are likely to entertain stereotypes about the person who carried out a theft or a burglary.

Responses to crime must not only meet the needs of victims but address the behaviour of offenders. Without subverting the criminal justice process as provided by the state, we need to find ways for both victims and offenders to become more involved in the outcome of cases, so that victims' voices are heard and so that offenders can be encouraged to take responsibility. While some young people may, due to the nature of their crimes, have to be removed from the community there is a real danger of constructing a fortress mentality—the notion that prison works. We should not be apologetic about creating a threshold of tolerance in communities that encourages the probation service, social services and others to develop community based penalties that are inclusive (ie which operate within the community) rather than exclusive (ie such as young offender institutions and secure training centres which exist outside of it), that integrate rather than stigmatise, that hold offenders to account rather than blame others for what they have done.

Such a regenerative process is often messy, complicated and fitful in terms of engaging the motivation and co-operation of a young person, but the opportunities for growth and fulfilment in the community are always likely to be more promising than the confined and alienating world of custody.

Notes

[1] S Millham, cited from a speech to the Association of Chief Probation Officers AGM, March 1993, London.

[2] D West and D Farrington, *Delinquency, its Roots and Careers* (Cambridge, 1977).

[3] A Hagell and T Newburn, 'Persistent Young Offenders', Policy Studies Institute (London, 1994).

[4] G McIvor, Sanctions for Serious and Persistent Offenders: A Review of the Literature, (Stirling University, 1990).

[5] G McIvor, (1990).

[6] R Coates *et al.*, *Diversity in Youth Correctional Services* (Cambridge, Massachusetts: Ballinger, 1978).

[7] R Coates *et al* (1978).

[8] D Farrington, 'Delinquency Prevention in the First Few Years of Life', *Justice of the Peace*, Vol 158, No 34 (1994).

[9] D Andrews & J Keissling, 'Programme Structure and Effective Correctional Practices', in R Ross & P Gendreau eds, *Effective Correctional Treatment* (Butterworth: Toronto, 1980).

CHAPTER 9

Prisoners' Children: Symptom of a Failing Justice System

Roger Shaw

The criminal justice system is based on principles of right and wrong, of acquitting the innocent and punishing the guilty—and only the guilty. Consequently, it cannot afford to consider what happens to the innocent families of prisoners because any recognition of their plight strikes at the very foundation of the system, namely that the innocent are not punished. Those responsible for legislation and for the implementation of our laws cannot, therefore, allow themselves to consider the implications posed by prisoners' families and the disruption to their relationships, let alone the impact which that has on their children's quality of life and future destiny. Such questions raise issues which, although simple to ask, are extremely difficult to answer. As a result, children of prisoners are sacrificed to the system and become the hidden victims of crime.

The concept of Relational Justice challenges this. It suggests that by dealing only with the offender and incarcerating him or her, his or her family environment worsens, as does the opportunity to exist productively and usefully in the outside world. The high reconviction rate of people released from prison is evidence of this and the plight of prisoners' children suggests that a proportion of them will follow in their fathers' footsteps, or in some cases in their mothers' footsteps.

Present realities
The numbers involved are not small. Shaw[1] demonstrated that every year in England and Wales in excess of 100,000 children experience the incarceration of their father. A third of the children in his samples were encountering this for the first time. Thus year on year figures suggest that at any one time more than half a million children under 16 years of age will have experienced their father imprisoned during the course of their childhood.

The number of children whose mothers are sent into custody each year is not accurately known and cannot be calculated simply on the basis that

114

the number of women received into prison annually is around 5 per cent of total prison receptions. There is a tendency for some lone mothers to hide the fact that they have children. Sometimes they leave them with friends and relatives if they are likely to go to prison because they fear that they may be seen as bad mothers and that their children will be taken into care and will not be returned to them when they are released. However accurate this belief, which is held by many mothers in prison, it is certainly indicative of an over-riding feeling about justice and social service systems. Whilst these systems ignore the child's needs when the parent is sentenced, particular interest is taken when that parent is released, even to the extent that the child may be removed from its natural mother and family home.

One can conclude that whilst the exact number of children in England and Wales who experience a parent imprisoned during their childhood is not known, it is considerable, somewhere between five per cent and ten per cent of the entire child population. It may only be a few days imprisonment for non-payment of fines or it may be a long-term or even a life sentence for grave matters. In Scotland, the proportion of the nation's children so affected is probably higher due to the greater use of short sentences of custody and more frequent imprisonment for fine default in that jurisdiction. Sometimes incarceration of a parent for a short period is more damaging because of the probability that the facts will be hidden from the child who may subsequently find out the real situation from other sources, such as peers at school, or from the newspaper or neighbours, thereby creating fears about what terrible thing the parent has done that cannot be talked about or is denied. This is potentially damaging to the relationship between the child and its parent and the trust which is so crucial for healthy development. An actual and not untypical case went thus:

A father was sent to prison for a few months for offences under the Theft Act. Mother told the eleven year old boy that father was working on an oil rig and would not be home for some months. The lad was quite prepared to accept this until a 'knowing' lad at school from a problem family, whose father was also in prison, announced to all and sundry, that 'Jimmy's dad's in the slammer'. Jimmy went home to ask his mother about this, to be told, 'Don't listen to that sort of rubbish, go upstairs and clean your teeth and get ready for bed'. This Jimmy duly did, to then lie in bed, churn things over in his mind, wonder what terrible thing Dad had done that mother could not talk about it and whether, in fact, he would ever see his father again. Other children at school got to hear of this as did their parents and before long Jimmy's peer group changed and he was left to mix only with the more troublesome boys. Very soon he, like them, was in trouble, convicted of burglary and identified as a criminal. The system, the community, and 'justice' had failed the vulnerable youngster.

The attitude of neighbours and acquaintances to a sentence of imprisonment of one of their members varies greatly according to the mores of the locality and the sub-culture of the area. In some instances, where it is the norm for families to have a member in prison or know of other families who have, people will come to the assistance of each other, even to the point of amplifying hostility towards the police and the system for what has happened and denying the fact that a crime has been committed. Elsewhere, there may be antagonism to the point of vindictiveness against the family members. Women have reported petrol soaked rags pushed through their letterboxes and children being attacked. One little boy whose father had been imprisoned was left crying, injured in the gutter. This action was perpetrated by neighbours who rationalised that they were 'upholding the law', and 'teaching a lesson'.

Teachers reported prisoners' children failing to concentrate, under-performing and giving indications of deep-seated unhappiness and rejection. Health Visitors identified babies failing to thrive and mothers unable to cope when support was removed by the incarceration of the male partner.[2] These and other studies, in what is now a growing body of research, show that imprisonment of a parent is usually bad for the family as a whole and bad for the children in particular. Where it can be avoided it is in the child's best interest to do so. It is probably in the best interest of society as well.

However, it may not be sufficient to suggest that—in the spirit of justice and in the 'child's best interests'—the courts should consider seriously what will happen to the family if they send someone to prison. Probably about half of all men received into prison have no stable relationships in the community. Should they be disadvantaged as a result and sent to prison when someone with an identical offence but who has a family would be left in the community? That may not be in the interests of justice either and cannot be seriously considered—or can it?

Punishing the innocent

If we return to the opening words of this chapter, namely that the foundation of our system is that the innocent are not punished, only the guilty, what alternative have we for ensuring that the children of prisoners are not made victims by the very system which upholds the law? Accept for a moment, for the purposes of debate, that offenders can be treated differently according to their family situation. How serious has an individual's behaviour to be before he or she is denied, and more importantly his children are denied, the relationship which is known to be so important for future destiny and stability?

What happens to the family matters. Not only does it matter for straight humanitarian reasons but it matters because the sentence was passed as a punishment on the criminal, not as a punishment on his or her

116

children. The damage which can be done to relationships between a child and its imprisoned parent was not part of that sentence and indeed it would be most unlikely for the court even to have contemplated this as a proper punishment when the sentence of imprisonment was passed. Courts already consider the background of offenders, their employment situation and other factors too, so why not the impact of a sentence on others? This is particularly important when it might be more severe on the innocent family members than was the offence on the victim in the first place! If this sounds rather trite, one only has to look at the reasons why many men are imprisoned for short periods, and women too, and then consider what happens to their children. For instance:

A single parent whose wife had died some years before was imprisoned for non-payment of fines. His two children were taken into care and separated into different children's homes whilst he was serving his time. Not only had they lost their mother, but then their father, their home and even their friends. They were then placed in a hostile environment as if they themselves were delinquent, as indeed were many of the other children with whom they were housed.

In another case:

A woman whose husband had deserted, was sent to prison for social security fraud. All the indications from neighbours and the health visitor were that she had been a good mother under very difficult circumstances but when she was sent to prison her child was taken into care by social services and was not returned for some time after her release. When eventually she was judged fit to have the child back, the change in the behaviour of the child was clear for all to see. A previously outward, happy and trusting little girl had become resentful, hostile, untrusting and insecure.

These two examples are not unique. In Shaw's study and in other studies a sufficient number of like cases emerged to indicate very worrying and damaging, although totally unintended, consequences resulting from the imprisonment of parents.

Relationships between prisoners and their families on the outside are critical and it behoves us all to enable those relationships to grow and to blossom. It is not a satisfactory answer to say 'the prisoner should have thought about that before he or she engaged in his or her criminal behaviour'. Such a shallow and irresponsible response, often heard from people who ought to know better, does not help the child.

Relational injustice

What is clear from the examples given in this paper is that the criminal justice system is operating in a way which ignores the importance of relationships. Its very activities help to sever one of the most important human relationships, that between a child and its parent and whilst it purports to 'punish the guilty and acquit the innocent' its effect is often the reverse. This has long been so and the multiplicity of traditions, beliefs, prejudices and pragmatic political expedients which impinge on the justice system have denied it a central focus for a clear policy. Recently, that state of affairs has worsened. In his presidential address to the Central Probation Council, the Hon Sir Patrick Garland identified 'the fundamental need for a properly thought out, cohesive approach to legislation in the criminal law and the philosophy underlying the approach to sentencing'.[3]

Justice is a community responsibility, with community obligations. But it is certainly not clear from the way in which justice is managed whether those obligations are even recognised and understood, let alone implemented. The constant striving for consistency in sentencing—when there is no consistency in any other part of the system—is but a cover for a framework which not only fails to bring either justice or crime reduction in its wake, but probably worsens matters by damaging human relationships, community spirit and trust. The criminal justice system is not about justice. How can it be when it separates out a tiny minority of the population and then by its actions, albeit unintended, harms their children? How can it be when the same society in any other arena articulates the responsibility which the community and adults have for the young of the species? A tiny minority indeed; with less than four per cent of known crimes resulting in a caution or conviction.[4] Some of those who support the present system would argue that those who are not brought to justice represent only minor offenders and petty transgressors but this is not the case. One has only to take two particularly serious crimes, arson and murder, to see that it is probable that only a small proportion of perpetrators are brought to justice.

Arson is one of the more damaging crimes, frequently having repercussions far exceeding those intended by the fire-raiser. It can readily lead to death, injury, loss of jobs and mistrust of institutions associated with insurance and business upon which much of the structure of society today rests. Yet it is believed that only two per cent of malicious or fraudulent fire raisers are brought to court.[5] Where murder is concerned one only has to look at the extent of the missing persons list to ponder the fate of at least some of those individuals and wonder whether the revelations in Gloucester in 1994, where it was reported that a number of bodies of missing persons were found buried in a building, is a unique incident or the tip of some iceberg. Possibly it lies somewhere in between.

The system, therefore, operates a highly refined and filtered mechanism. Its various imperfections and inadequacies ensure that only a tiny minority of offenders—most of whom are economically disadvantaged—are prosecuted and where they are judged to require a custodial sentence their families and children are punished too; sacrificed to a failing justice system.

Scapegoats

A question therefore arises. If the justice system is not about justice, except in name, what is it about? Certainly it is about retribution and as far as some offenders are concerned that is right and proper if the community is to feel sufficiently avenged so as not to have to take the law into its own hands. In this respect the minority of offenders who are brought to justice are but ritual sacrifices to meet this end. The justice system also marks the boundary between acceptable and unacceptable behaviour, again a perfectly reasonable role. Importantly also, where a serious offender is locked up securely the public is protected from his or her dangerous or disruptive behaviour.

If the ambitions for the system were simple and stopped there they might be less vulnerable to criticism. However, those ambitions go beyond that. The claim is much grander, ie the reduction of crime. Here the system patently fails as the few statistics given in this chapter show. There is now much evidence to demonstrate the ineffectiveness of imprisonment as a method of crime reduction. For instance, following their study of crime and punishment in England and Wales and in the USA in the 1980s Farrington and Langan[6] concluded that 'existing evidence does not suggest that crime can be dramatically reduced simply by putting more offenders behind bars. Modest reductions in crime may be possible, but major and lasting reductions in crime probably will require social intervention techniques, such as parent training or pre-school intellectual enrichment programmes'. In terms of punishment it fails to distinquish between different individuals in society who may suffer disproportionately from the penalties meted out. For instance, a fine is only a minor matter to a wealthy person but significant to one of limited means. Imprisonment for some social classes has a different impact to that on others and a different effect according to the gender of the person concerned, their occupation and their age.

Similarly, prisons vary. An individual may be in an institution relatively close to home or a great distance from it. This will influence the punitive effect of the prison sentence on both the prisoner and his or her family, whilst being usually uninfluenced by the nature of the crime which was committed. In any case, a person is sent to prison as a punishment and not to be punished. Our prisons do not only vary in their distance from the offender's home. Some are old, overcrowded, Victorian institutions, cramped, unhygienic and degrading whilst others, by comparison, are uncrowded, relatively comfortable and in pleasant environments. The criteria used in allocating a prisoner to an establishment is primarily concerned with security and whether there are any vacancies. The needs of the family noted in the Woolf Report[7] are seldom addressed seriously.

However one looks at the present criminal justice system, whether it be acquitting the innocent, punishing only those guilty of crimes rather than the family, protecting the public, reducing crime, reinforcing the stability of society or seeming to be fair and just, one can only come to the conclusion that it is failing to such an extent that if its performance was replicated in other arenas, such as business, it would not be tolerated. People are not protected by it, victims are seldom helped by it and crime is not prevented as we lurch from one political or financial expedient to another. Meanwhile, the tiny proportion of criminals who are captured and imprisoned are made scapegoats and their family units are strained or destroyed. Many children are emotionally damaged and the foundations for future behavioural problems may be laid down. The growth of insecurity and fear, mistrust and resentment, delinquency and crime, is guaranteed.

One of the principal difficulties with which the system has to contend is that of dealing with the perceived expectations of the public. These are largely associated with punishment on the one hand and reducing crime on the other. These two expectations, retribution and rehabilitation, do not sleep comfortably in the same bed. What is regarded as appropriate and adequate punishment is usually incompatible with what one might choose to do to rehabilitate someone or help them to see themselves accepted by others as a useful members of the community. Imprisonment has been shown not to be effective in changing patterns of criminal behaviour.

Indeed, if an Intelligence with no knowledge of earthly things came down from Outer-space and viewed the justice systems of the developed nations and saw how we gathered the vulnerable, those with poor social skills and little education but with some experience of delinquency and herded them together in institutions with other disadvantaged people and a sprinkling of serious criminals, then to release them at a later date, possibly to no home, probably to no job and definitely to be labelled by the outside world as jailbirds and criminals, the Intelligence might be forgiven for thinking we were actually trying to *increase* crime, rather than reduce it. He, she or it would not have to engage in very much serious research to demonstrate that this is *exactly* what we are doing!

In areas of high crime and delinquency it is now the norm for communities to have within them a significant proportion of people with prison experience. In those areas it is the norm for children to grow up having experienced, if not of their own father imprisoned, then the father of one of their friends.[8]

Thus the most serious penalty that the state can mete out becomes commonplace. Whether it is a few days for non-payment of a fine or many years for a serious criminal matter, it is still imprisonment with similar impact on the trust, feelings and worries of the community. In research studies, children who knew their father was in prison saw it simply as that. Seldom was it justified in terms of not having paid a fine for failure to return a library book or not having a television licence. As one teacher explained 'imprisonment of a parent is either stigma or status. Whatever the reason for the sentence the local social norms determine the attitude and result.'[9] Whatever the reason it identifies the child and causes an adjustment in the child's peer group and consequently to his or her attitude to the community, the community's attitude to the child and the subsequent learned behaviour which results.

Perhaps the time has come when we should move away from an offender-focused system and consider the community, victims and relationships. Surveys show that the public is not as punitive as some who purport to speak on its behalf would have us believe. A move towards a victim-oriented model, that considered the hidden victims of crime and which embodied concepts of Relational Justice, may be overdue.

Notes

[1] R Shaw, *Children of Imprisoned Fathers* (London: Hodder & Stoughton, 1987). See also: J Matthews, *Forgotten Victims* (London. NACRO, 1983); B Hounslow, A Stephenson, J Stewartt and T Crancher, *Children of Imprisoned Parents* (Australia, Ministry of Youth and Community Services of New South Wales).

[2] R. Shaw, *Prisoners' Children: What are the Issues?* (London: Routledge, 1992).

[3] P. Garland (17 May 1994) *President's address to Central Probation Council.*, London: AGM.

[4] Home Office, *British Crime Survey 1992*, Hors 132 (London: HMSO, 1993).

[5] Arson Prevention Bureau (1994) *Arson Investigation Seminar, 25/26 April 1994*, London.

[6] D Farrington and P Langan, 'Changes in Crime and Punishment in England and America in the 1980s', *Justice Quarterly*, (1992).

[7] Lord Justice Woolf, *Report of an Inquiry into Prison Disturbance April 1990* (London: HMSO, 1991), Command 1456.

[8] Shaw, *Prisoners' Children: What are the Issues?* (1992).

[9] R Shaw, Personal correspondence following survey of teachers' experiences of children with imprisoned fathers (1986).

CHAPTER 10

My Brother's Keeper: Relationships in Prison

Andrew Coyle

I have visited prisons in many countries across the world. I have come away from some of these visits full of amazement at man's ability to rise above his conditions and to display the best aspects of humanity in even the most deprived circumstances. At the end of other visits I have been utterly depressed at man's inhumanity to his fellow man, at the complete absence of any vestige of dignity or respect. Sometimes these extreme sentiments have been experienced in different prisons in the same country.

Humanity and inhumanity

In one country of the former Soviet bloc I visited a women's prison where the cowed prisoners were dressed in shifts made of a serge material with vertical stripes. It was a replica of the uniforms worn by prisoners in concentration camps during the Second World War. The similarities did not end there. The single shower room in the prison was a large barn-like building, completely bare apart from forty shower heads which protruded from the ceiling. The place reeked of the shame and humiliation which must have been felt by these women each week as they went to the large ante-room, took off all their clothes and then were herded into this shower room. In all probability the guards did not set out to be cruel or to degrade. They simply no longer saw the humanity and the individuality of the women for whom they had responsibility. In becoming prisoners the women had been stripped of their dignity as human beings.

Another prison held twelve hundred young men aged between fourteen and 18 years. It was officially described as a 'School of Re-education and Rehabilitation'. The young men were accommodated in large dormitories, with bunk-beds crammed together. The young people spent most of each day locked in these dormitories. There was one member of staff for every five dormitories. Official sources assured us that there was no physical or sexual abuse. Unofficial sources told quite a different story. The youngsters had no personal possessions. Their heads were shaved and they wore long grey greatcoats as a protection against the biting cold. The director and his staff gave the impression of being reasonably caring people but they were faced with an impossible task.

This form of inhumanity was direct and almost palpable. In other countries it is more indirect but nonetheless real. In several high security prisons in North America there is no physical contact between prisoners and guards. Staff observe the prisoners through bullet proof glass and control their movement through electronic doors, speaking to them only with the use of microphones. The prisoners spend their days in concrete boxes. On the odd occasion when they have to leave their zoo they are handcuffed and shackled and escorted by armed guards.

These examples have to be balanced against other quite different situations in which staff work quite closely with prisoners in a positive manner. There are many instances, for example, in which prisoners and staff, despite their different circumstances, combine to help old or handicapped people or take on projects to help their community.

In objective terms there is no such thing as a 'good' prison. However necessary, they are always abnormal institutions in which one group of human beings deprives another group of human beings of liberty. So what distinguishes a decent and humane prison from one which is cruel and degrading? It is not merely the physical condition of the buildings nor the material resources. Some of the most inhuman prisons in the world have superb physical conditions and state of the art security devices.

The most important feature distinguishing a prison which is decent from one which is not is the nature of the human relations which exist within it. These will operate at many levels: between staff and prisoners, prisoners and prisoners, staff and staff, the prison community and the outside community.

Keepers and kept

Given the choice between a new, state of the art prison run by a rigid, unprofessional staff and a run down set of buildings with a highly committed, dedicated staff, a wise prison governor would invariably choose the latter. Obviously the ideal would be to have good buildings and a good staff. But if it were an option between one and the other, there really would be no choice to be made.

The task of the first line prison officer is one of the most complex jobs imaginable. Society, through the courts, has decided that certain human beings have to be deprived of liberty. The prison officer enforces that decision. So, at the most basic level, one can say that the task of the prison officer is to lock people up. But that is only the beginning. The next thing is that the prison officer has to be careful not to be judgmental about the men and women who are in his or her care. There is a great temptation that staff, particularly those who deal directly with prisoners, will be seduced into thinking that because they wear a different style of uniform they are better people than the men and women they look after.

It is abnormal that one set of human beings should have what at times is virtually complete control over what another set of human beings can do, even to the extent of deciding when they may attend to their bodily functions. It is important to distinguish this power over what a person does from power over the person himself or herself. It is possible for one human being to surrender power over himself or herself to another person or body. It is not possible for that power to be taken by force. Nor, in the prison setting, should any attempt be made to achieve this.

One of the tasks of prison staff is to give prisoners an opportunity to reinforce their dignity as human beings, both for their own sakes and for that of society. One feature which characterizes many prisoners is a lack of self-esteem; a life experience which has led them to conclude that they have nothing to offer to society and can expect nothing from it in return. From an early stage many of them have been told that they are failures: by their parents, by their teachers, by their church if they have one, by their employer if they have one. By ending up in prison they have failed even in their criminality.

That is not to deny that many people who are in prison have committed terrible acts for which there can be no justification. But one has to distinguish between what a person is and what a person does. Only in this way can one ensure that requiring decency, fairness and justice for the offender does not involve deserting the victim who has been injured by the crime which has been committed.

There are other important features to keep in mind. One is that there is often a very fine line between an offender and a victim. Most offenders are young men in their late teens or early twenties. Many victims, particularly of violent crimes, come from the same group. A victim one day may be an offender the next.

Another is that a significant proportion of men and women who are in prison in the United Kingdom are not major criminals. About one quarter of them are on remand and have yet to be found guilty of any offence. Of this group, the majority will not subsequently receive a custodial sentence.

In some countries prison staff are little more than guards. Their main task is to ensure that prisoners do not escape and that acts of indiscipline are kept to a minimum. Little attention is paid to what happens within the walls of the prison. In some instances staff will be brutal and inhumane in their dealings with prisoners. In many cases it will simply be a matter of indifference to their situation.

A prison is not a sensitive place. Sensitivity may well be interpreted as weakness, any display of emotion is likely to be mocked. Prison never will be, and never can be, an equal society. It takes a considerable degree of personal maturity on the part of each member of staff to recognise the humanity in each man and woman who is in prison. And a great deal of professional confidence.

The officer who is uncertain, who lacks the strength of personality to influence prisoners may hide behind the power of his or her uniform, may seek to exercise his or her responsibilities by a direct and impersonal order rather than in a more positive manner. In the long term this will be insufficient.

The key players in any prison are the prisoner and the front line prison officer. The latter is the one person in the system who will have the greatest influence for better or for worse on the prisoner. The wise officer knows that security and good order are not in conflict with the principles of good human relations, of treating prisoners decently and humanely. On the contrary, the two sets of requirements complement each other. Security and good order will be strengthened in an establishment in which the staff know the prisoners and encourage them to take part in the various activities and programmes which are offered. The prisoner's perspective of what happens when respect for the prisoner as human being is forgotten was given in a letter which a prisoner sent to Lord Justice Woolf (as he then was) in the course of his inquiry into the riot at Strangeways Prison, Manchester:

> It is obvious if prisoners are treated like animals, sworn at, degraded and psychologically toyed with week after week, they in turn lose respect, not only for their tormentors, but for society at large.[1]

The prisoner as person

It is too easy for us to think of men and women who are in prison as somehow being a race apart. It is as if the fact that they are deprived of their liberty means that they have lost their common humanity. From time to time people who have no prior experience of the prison system will have occasion to visit a prison. It is not unusual at the end of such a visit to hear a comment to the effect that the prisoners 'look so ordinary', almost as though the visitor thought that they would be physically different from other human beings.

It is important to remember that prisoners are not a homogeneous group. The main common feature which they have is that they are in prison, either accused or convicted of having committed a criminal offence. In respect of everything else they are as heterogeneous a group of human beings as one might wish to encounter. In a large prison for men, the majority of prisoners will be quite young, in their early or mid-twenties, but there will be a smattering of older men or women. Many will be parents, wishing to retain close links with their children and with other members of their families. Some will be professional men or women, others will be tradesmen or unskilled. In recent years many of them will have been unemployed. Many will have little or no educational qualifications but some will be highly educated. In an inner city prison there will be a cosmopolitan mix, with men from many countries and cultures.

Almost 97 per cent of the people who are in prison in England and Wales are men. The first thing which is done to a man when he comes into prison is that he is stripped of his individuality, both literally and metaphorically. His clothes are taken from him, he is given a bath or shower, which is as much a symbolic washing as anything else. He is given a set of prison uniform clothing, which is quite likely to be second-hand. And he is given a number which, throughout the time he is in prison, will be virtually more important than his name.

He is then taken to a cell, a small room, furnished with a bunk bed, a table and a chair. If the prison is for remand prisoners or those who have recently been convicted he will probably have to share the cell with a complete stranger. He will soon get to know his new companion because they will be locked in that small room for much of the day and the whole night. Even in the mid-1990s in the United Kingdom he may have access to sanitation only if a member of staff allows him out of his cell. At other times he may have to make use of a small plastic chamber pot to perform his bodily functions while his companion turns discreetly away. If one of the two men lies on the bunk bed, the other will be able to take six steps between the window and the door, a door with no handle on the inside.

It is difficult for someone who has never been a prisoner to imagine what it must be like to be deprived of liberty. To have no power over where one goes or what one does. To be dependent on permission from other people for everything, perhaps even the frequency with which one goes to the toilet. The real world becomes something different, something separated. A new world is created in which minor details take on great significance. Vaclav Havel, the President of the Czech Republic, was imprisoned in Czechoslovakia in 1979. In the course of a series of letters written from prison to his wife he described what it was like to be in prison:

> I used to think prison life must be endless boredom and monotony with nothing much to worry about except the basic problem of making the time pass quickly. But now I've discovered it's not like that. You have plenty of worries here all the time, and though they may seem 'trivial' to the normal

world, they are not at all trivial in the prison context. In fact you're always having to chase after something, hunt for something, keep an eye on something, fear for something, hold your ground against something, etc. It's a constant strain on the nerves, (someone is always twanging on them), exacerbated by the fact that in many important instances you cannot behave authentically and must keep your real thoughts to yourself.[2]

In a male setting it is sometimes suggested that being in prison holds little fear for someone who has been at boarding school or in the armed forces. That comparison is superficial. It is true in so far as one is never alone, there is no privacy, there is always someone to give directions or orders. It is not true in other important respects. Neither oneself nor one's companions have chosen to be there and, given the opportunity, everyone would leave. There is no shared objective or common purpose. When release does come there will be no sense of camaraderie nor of wishing to return for the occasional reunion.

Generally speaking prisoners care little about the prison system. Even in long-term prisons it is difficult to engage prisoners in a debate about how the system should be run or how it might be improved. What concerns prisoners is what is happening to them in prison. How their lot might be improved. How the pain of their imprisonment might be lessened.

As in every society there is a pecking order in the world of the prison. Usually one's place within this is determined by the crime of which one has been convicted or with which one is charged. People who have committed serious crimes such as armed robbery tend to be at the top of the pecking order. At the bottom are those who have committed crimes of a sexual nature. If the victim of the crime has been a child or an old person, the offender is regarded as beneath contempt. Not only that, other prisoners will feel quite entitled to wreak whatever vengeance they can on such men. This highly judgmental, almost moralistic attitude is much more pronounced in the United Kingdom than in most other countries. One can speculate why this should be so. The manner in which every grisly detail of such offences is reported in certain sections of the press, often accompanied by an emotional outburst about what should be done to the offender, leaves other prisoners enthusiastic to take on the role of vigilante.

Whatever the reason, prisoners who have been convicted of crimes of this nature have to be physically protected from other prisoners by being held in separate units. Ironically, this has led to a move to provide courses which oblige them to face up to their behaviour in a direct manner. These courses probably would not have been developed so quickly had these prisoners not been held apart in a discrete group.

Occasionally one comes across examples of great generosity among prisoners. It may be when someone suffers the bereavement of a close family member or friend, a particularly difficult experience for a man or woman deprived of liberty. It may be when a person who is clearly mentally disturbed comes into prison for the first time and more experienced prisoners ease his way. It may come from an older man who sees a headstrong youngster about to embark on a lifetime of knocking his head against the system, just as he had done 20 years before, and who takes him under his wing to prevent this happening. Examples such as these, which occur more often than one might expect, serve to remind us of the human being who lives within the uniform of the prisoner.

More than a cog in the machine
If the prison system is a great machine, the prison officer is frequently regarded as the cog in that machine. Often little respected, frequently not even noticed, the prison officer is the man or woman without whom the whole system would grind to a halt. Until recently little attention was paid to the uniformed prison officer by senior management or by those outside the service. But prisoners were never in any doubt that the person who could influence their daily life to a far greater extent than any governor or administrator was the officer on the landing, who opened up the cell doors first thing in the morning and who locked them up last thing at night.

What sort of person wants to earn his or her living by locking up other human beings? In many countries prison staff are drawn from the ranks of retired members of the armed services. This reflects the military hierarchy which still permeates many prison systems. Men and women who have been accustomed to working in a disciplined environment which demands consistent obedience to orders and requires little in the way of initiative are understandably attracted to what they perceive to be a similar way of working.

This pattern of recruitment to the prison system has changed significantly in the United Kingdom over the last three decades. Young men and women who join the prison service today come from all walks of life. Some will have been unemployed; some will have been tradesmen or teachers. Some will have basic educational qualifications; others will have a university degree. The work of the prison officer is relatively secure and offers a good starting salary given that no professional qualifications are required.

A young man or woman about to embark on a career in the prison service is given relatively little training for the very complex job which lies ahead. After an initial training period of no more than a few months he or she is let loose on the landings of a prison, often to look after 50 or 60 prisoners. During the first year there is a degree of individual supervision from senior staff. Inevitably during the complexity of daily interaction with prisoners the young officer is left largely to use his or her own initiative. It is difficult to hide behind the security of the official uniform. There is an informality on the landings which makes this impossible. The officer has to exert authority by strength of personality and persuasion.

The relationship between uniformed staff and senior management in the prison service has frequently been a stormy one. Officers have sometimes been unclear about what is expected of them. The complementary nature of security and good order on the one hand and positive relations between officers and prisoners on the other has not always been clear. Instead they have been perceived as alternatives. One can have good security or positive regimes, so the argument goes, but not both. Management has sometimes been less supportive of staff as it requires them to achieve an extremely complex balance in their daily work.

The prison and the community

Many of the men and women in prison have been convicted of minor offences and are serving relatively short sentences. It is not helpful to refer to prisons, which hold human beings, as the 'dustbins' of our society but one can understand the frustration which leads to that description. Our over-organised, highly pressured society measures success largely in terms of material possessions and is very critical of what it considers to be failure. People who are regarded as inconvenient, either because of their lifestyle or because of their inability to cope, are to be swept out of our consciousness, behind the high wall of the prison, with little thought being given to the reality that they will shortly be back in our community again.

The roots of imprisonment lie in the notion of exile from the community. The Victorian fortress prisons, many of which are still in use today, were built when transportation to the colonies came to an end. Their high walls were built in order to keep the community out as well as to keep prisoners in.

In practice, prisons have never existed in a vacuum nor in total isolation from the rest of society. This notion is certainly not acceptable today. Prisons exist because society wants them to. The community has not only the right but also the obligation to know what goes on in its prisons. In the terminology of today, prison walls should be permeable. This means that, having taken due account of security considerations, whenever possible prisoners should be allowed temporary release from prison in order to prepare themselves for eventual return to the community by getting work experience and training or by helping people who are more disadvantaged than they are. At the same time, members of the community should be encouraged to come into prison to work with prisoners, to counsel them and to join in organised activities with them.

This is not a soft option. It is a recognition that almost all prisoners, even those who are serving very long sentences, will one day return to the community. If they are not to come out more bitter than when they went in and more likely to commit further crime, they must be encouraged to develop a sense of personal worth and a realisation that they can contribute to the community, that they are valued human beings.

Notes

[1] Lord Justice Woolf, *Report of an Inquiry into Prison Disturbances, April 1990* (London: HMSO, 1991), Command 1456.
[2] V Havel, *Letters to Olga* (London: Faber and Faber, 1990).

Part III

Convictions and Values

11 Believing in Justice
Christopher Townsend

12 Repairing the Breach: A Personal Motivation
Peter Walker

CHAPTER 11

Believing in Justice

Christopher Townsend

It is a commonplace that we live in a multi-faith society. Notwithstanding the impact of a long process of secularisation, the majority of people in modern Britain still claim some adherence to Christian beliefs, and several religions enjoy the support of a significant number of active practitioners. That fact creates a challenge and an opportunity. The challenge is to sustain a civic society that respects the differences between faith communities and facilitates their peaceful co-existence. Our criminal justice system should, ideally, operate in a way that is capable of earning the respect of members of each of these faith communities, even though wholehearted endorsement is likely to be impossible. The opportunity, at a time when secular values often look threadbare, arises from the resources within the traditions of ethical reflection represented by the faith communities.

This chapter contains some reflections on justice drawn from the scriptures which underlie the three great monotheistic religions of the world: Judaism, Christianity and Islam. The ethical resources of each religion naturally go beyond their scriptures. The Talmud (a compendium of rabbinic reflection), the writings of the Church Fathers, the Hadith (sacred sayings of Mohammed), and much besides, are all relevant. Indeed Jews and Muslims and some Christians would regard certain texts as vital companions to the scriptures if a thoroughly Jewish, Islamic or, as the case may be, Christian perspective is to be developed. Nonetheless, in each religion the scriptures have a certain primacy over subsequent complementary and derivative texts and resources. For this reason, we focus on the scriptures and, indeed, this material alone has a richness that can only be hinted at here.

The scriptures owe their pre-eminence to the fact that, notwithstanding the role of human prophets and scribes in their production and transmission, they are (or have for centuries been) regarded as the very words of God. Nonetheless, when we read the scriptures we find ourselves eavesdropping on communities from a different era. The distance between us and them in terms of worldview, culture and context is great—even for people who share the same religion. These ancient communities contain features we would not wish to emulate. However, at a deep level, the experience of human living has not changed. These scriptures bear witness to principles relevant to an understanding and application of justice. Some are already in full bloom, some are seeds still to grow, but all are thought-provoking and, in many cases, attractive. The quest for justice is as old as the hills. Our present age is unrivalled in its technological competence but it would be a mistake to assume that the same is necessarily true of the depth, insight and balance of our moral reflection. We shall find we have things to learn from as well as to criticise.

None of the religions under consideration is characterized by a monolithic unity. Each contains various branches and schools of thought with significant differences of emphasis. Readers with an intimate knowledge of one or other of these religions will be able to identify which emphases are being overlooked. A single chapter must, inevitably, be selective.

Orthodox versions of Judaism, Christianity and Islam each claim to bear witness to truth in a unique way. The reader should be made aware (and might in any case have guessed before long) that my worldview is shaped by Christian convictions. In places this may have coloured my understanding of the witness of the Jewish and Islamic scriptures to the idea of justice even though my aim has been to represent, fairly and accurately, their distinctive perspectives.

The Hebrew scriptures

We may begin our exploration of justice in the Hebrew scriptures by considering four key words: *berith, tsedeq, mishpat* and *shalom*.

The covenant, or *berith*, between Yahweh and his people Israel provides the theological context for all that occurs within the life of Israel and all that is recorded in the Hebrew scriptures. God initiated a relationship with his chosen people Israel, by his promises to their father Abraham, by delivering them from Egypt, by committing himself to them and by giving them his law. The covenant gave an offence by an individual a significance for the community (for potentially it affected the relationship of the whole people with God) and a transcendent point of reference (for it was God's law being broken). An offence was understood not as an infraction of a social contract but a violation of the life of community before God. Ideas of crime, sin and guilt overlapped considerably and no clear distinction between civil and criminal law existed. One consequence of the 'concept of a covenant' is 'that all life and existence are seen in social, that is, historical terms of relationship and mutuality.'[1]

From an etymological perspective, the root meaning of *tsedeq*, often translated as righteousness, is 'straightness' in a physical sense. Thus it speaks of conformity to a norm. However, the word has a richness of meaning not adequately captured by any single word in English. But the core idea is a personal concept: it is essentially the fulfilment of the demands and obligations inherent in a relationship between two persons.[2] The Torah urges every individual Israelite 'Justice, justice shalt thou pursue'[3] using the words '*tsedeq, tsedeq*'.

Mishpat brings us more directly into the arena of criminal justice and includes within its range of meaning: law, judicial acts, and extra-judicial action for justice's sake.[4] C J H Wright has observed, helpfully, that when a wrong has been done '*mishpat* is what needs to be done if people and circumstances are to be restored to conformity with *tsedeq*'.[5]

Shalom encapsulates the Hebrew ideal for the life of the community. *Shalom* summarises the all-rightness of things which God intends. This is the dynamic peace of the community; fulfilment, wholeness, and right relationships between individuals, the community, and God. Its close link with the pursuit of justice is revealed by the Psalmist who anticipates with longing the day when righteousness (*tsedeq*) and peace (*shalom*) [shall] kiss each other'.[6] *Shalom* can arise only when justice infuses all areas of community life.

This brief review of key terms reveals that the understanding of justice in the Hebrew scriptures is not an abstract, impersonal concept but a highly personal and relational term. Little surprise, therefore, that a work on Jewish jurisprudence should say that 'Jewish law endeavours to be humane as well as just and, therefore, takes cognizance of the human element in all human relationship.'[7]

The Torah establishes principles which we now regard as axiomatic to true justice. Indeed, our convictions have been shaped, in part, by the historical influence of Jewish law through the spread of Christianity to Europe. There should be access to justice, equality before the law and fair judgments for all, including the poor and the immigrant, for Moses charged the judges he appointed:

> Hear the disputes between your brothers and judge fairly, whether the case is between brother Israelites or between one of them and an alien. Do not show partiality in judging; hear both small and great alike. Do not be afraid of any man, for judgment belongs to God.[8]

Likewise, the penalty for an offence was to be in proportion to its seriousness and a sustained distinction between intentional and unintentional crimes was upheld.

Throughout Israel's history, local administration of justice by the elders of the community gathered at the town gates had an important role. A case heard by the gathered elders would involve a forensic process culminating in a verdict: 'the judges will decide the case, acquitting the innocent and condemning the guilty'.[9] However, this process had a community emphasis as well. Judging rightly was not simply applying a formal standard of justice in an impartial way. The aim was 'to settle a dispute between members of the community so that prosperous co-existence was possible'.[10] If the administration of justice aimed at community well-being, it was also characterized by community responsibility and participation. If a 'public charge to testify regarding something [a person] has seen or learned about' was issued, failure to speak up was a 'sin' for which the person would 'be held responsible'.[11]

It was normally the injured party, or a close relative, and not an independent cadre of professionals, who reported the crime to the community elders and presented his or her case. In doing so he or she confronted the offender with his or her actions and their consequences. There was full opportunity, beforehand, to pursue non-judicial means of settling the dispute. Levels of required compensation appear lower where matters are settled without recourse to judicial procedures.[12] Litigants were urged not to neglect the normal requirements of brotherly obligation even though they were at odds at law.[13] The relationship was never to become one of sheer animosity or indifference. However, despite the standing obligation on an Israelite to love his neighbour as himself, the Torah never goes so far as to place victim and offender under a specific obligation to be reconciled, possibly a tacit recognition of the realities of the situation.

After the establishment of the monarchy in ancient Israel, the king acted in a judicial capacity and appointed judges in the towns.[14] Indeed 'The king was the fount of Justice'.[15] The ideal that the king was meant to embody is articulated in Psalm 72, sung at the enthronement of a new king:

Endow the king with your justice, O God, the royal son with your righteousness.
He will judge your people in righteousness, your afflicted ones with justice.[16]

These verses make plain that the ultimate source of justice was considered to be the just character of God. The Psalmist extols God saying 'Righteousness and justice are the foundation of your throne'.[17]

When a person was found guilty of a wrongful act and punished the key objectives included retribution, reparation and, typically, subsequent re-integration into the community.

An offender was to receive what his offence deserved. The severity of the punishment was to correspond with the gravity of his crime. The *lex talionis* ('an eye for an eye, a tooth for a tooth') is the most well-known expression of this principle. Far from being a harsh law, its purpose was to set a limit on the revenge a person might seek to exact. It was not a prescription for judicial mutilation but a symbolical measure of the appropriate amount of punishment and/or compensation the offender should give to the injured person.[18] Further, it appears to have acted as a maximum rather than mandatory level of punishment.

If a crime were sufficiently serious the course of action required to be taken by the community was exclusion of the offender from that community, by execution, excommunication or temporary 'exile' in a city of refuge. Capital punishment for murder was carried out by the next of kin, the *go'el haddam* (literally 'redeemer of blood'). In other cases, execution was normally by stoning. The prosecution witnesses cast the first stones and the people continued until the offender's death. 'The collective character of communal justice was thus expressed to the end.'[19] However, by comparison with neighbouring cultures, ancient Israel used the death penalty relatively rarely and only after exacting evidential requirements had been satisfied. The level of punishment imposed for different offences reflected the scale of values in the Torah. Blatant offences against God (a form of treason in a theocracy), certain actions that violated the integrity of the family and violent crimes against the person were punished severely.[20] No mere property crimes incurred the death penalty, a distinctive feature of Israel's penal system. By contrast, Mesopotamian law rated economic loss highly, assigning the death penalty to such offences as breaking and entering, looting at a fire, and theft.[21]

In most cases, the offender had to make restitution to the victim: with money, in kind or by labour. The offender was penalised and the victim compensated for inconvenience by adding between one-fifth[22] and four times[23] the amount of the original damage. The prominence of restitution and absence of fines payable to the community/state is one of the noteworthy contrasts between the patterns in the Torah and our present day arrangements. The themes of 'victim compensation' and 'offender responsibility' could, it might be suggested, be given more prominence today.

In most cases, once punishment/compensation had been carried out, the offender was fully re-integrated into society with no loss of civil rights. The importance of respect for offenders in their treatment was underlined. In cases where corporal punishment was adopted, the harshness of the punishment was limited so as to ensure that the offender (referred to as 'your brother') was not degraded.[24] Normally an offender was neither removed from the community nor separated from his family. One form of punishment nowhere mentioned in ancient Israel's law is imprisonment which has been described as 'expensive to the community, generally corrupting to the prisoner and often bringing unmerited hardship to his dependants . . . the invention of a later age'.[25]

Justice and punishment in Jewish thought and practice has always been, and is today, influenced by the ethical ideals of the Torah. Put positively, these ideals speak of compassion and committed loving-kindness. Put negatively, one summary was given by Hillel, a famous Pharisee and great teacher in the first century BCE, who 'when asked by a would-be convert to teach him the whole Torah while he stood on one foot replied: "What is hateful to you, do not do to your fellow man; that is the essence of the Torah, the rest is commentary: go and learn."'[26]

The New Testament

The cross on which Jesus Christ died is at the heart of the New Testament. The gospels, recording the early life and three years of ministry by Jesus, spend a third of their material on the betrayal, arrest, trial and execution of Jesus. The remainder of the New Testament looks back on the cross, not as a tragedy or heroic failure, but as the scene of Christ's greatest achievement. This was the decisive event by which Jesus revealed the extent of God's love for humankind, opened the door for people to enjoy a restored relationship with God and won his victory over the forces of evil. New Testament reflections on justice must be informed by a theology of the cross.

The Epistle to the Romans tells us that God gave up Christ to die on the cross 'to demonstrate his justice'.[27] Throughout the Hebrew scriptures, the Old Testament to Christians, God claims to be committed to justice and resolved to punish wrongdoing yet a glance at our world reveals many evil acts apparently overlooked. The wicked often prosper. This enigma, and the accusation of moral indifference on God's part, receive an answer at the cross. For here, God punished every human evil to the uttermost by punishing them in Christ.

The same verse goes on to say that through Christ's sacrifice on the cross God 'justifies those who have faith in Christ Jesus'.[28] Since the Reformation, the idea of justification has often been cast in forensic terms. Each person's status in God's eyes is one of guilt until he or she believes in Christ and is declared innocent. There is ample New Testament warrant for this imagery. However, the New Testament also builds on the Hebrew scriptures concept of righteousness as right relationship. Thus 'justified' can be taken to imply, even mean, 'being in right relation with God' and 'justification' speaks of the 'rectification' of a personal relationship. That right relationship is possible because God is willing, on account of

Christ's death, to forgive fully and freely, the human actions which first severed the relationship.

The New Testament emerged from a community which, unlike ancient Israel, was at no point a separate political entity. The state, with its role of apprehending and punishing lawbreakers, lay outside the Christian community. This creates complications when seeking to draw out possible implications of the cross for a criminal justice system. There are Christians who, seeing the cross as the place where mercy triumphs over the harsh demands of divine judgment, have urged the removal of any notion of retribution from criminal justice. However, the New Testament describes the person who is a ruler as 'God's servant, an agent of wrath to bring punishment on the wrongdoer'[29] and governors as 'sent by him [the Lord] to punish those who do wrong and to commend those who do right'.[30] So reflection about the cross must not overlook the fact that it reveals a determination not to ignore, but rather to address and, indeed, punish wrongdoing.

However, few if any Christians reflecting on the biblical witness have been content to advocate retributive justice alone. For example, Archbishop William Temple in *The Ethics of Penal Action* argued for an approach to punishment in which retribution, deterrence and reform are intertwined. Society has a moral duty to repudiate an offender's crime, reassert the broken laws and treat the offender as a responsible moral agent. Any deterrent effect this may have on others is a welcome practical benefit but morally justifiable only if subordinate to matters of desert and denunciation. Seeking reform of the offender is 'valuable in the sympathy which it exhibits and in the effects which it produces . . . it is also that which alone confers upon the [other] the full quality of justice'.[31] For if no attention is paid to the interests of the offender, punishment deteriorates into mere vengeance. This threefold approach involves a concern for the welfare of the community, prospective victims and the offender. However, as the following paragraphs show, further reflections about the cross can both intensify and complement this threefold concern.

The experience of the cross, Jesus suffering as the victim of an unfair trial, treated as a criminal, and subjected to excruciating pain, underpins Christian concern for those who are victims and those who are punished. The example of Jesus, who lived and died as 'the man for others', serves as an inspiration to seek the welfare of people, not least those who are undeserving and unable to help themselves.

The necessity of the cross affects the Christian attitude towards offenders. The cross was unavoidable in God's purposes because of the divine verdict on the human condition: 'all have sinned and fall short of the glory of God'.[32] The New Testament is aware that, in human and relative terms, people may be good or bad. However, one of its basic presuppositions is that there is one tribunal at which every person's life will be found badly wanting. The belief that 'all have sinned' leaves no place for despising offenders. Judge and convict, prison officer and inmate, all ultimately share a common humanity in which both measureless dignity and profound shame are to be found. God values each person so much that he gave up his only Son for our sake; our redemption required Christ's death because no other remedy could deal with the extent of our moral failure.

The achievement of the cross was the possibility of renewed relationship between God and humankind. The death and resurrection of Christ led, moreover, to the formation of a new community. Thus, in God's initiative at the cross, punishment of wrongdoing springing from the demands of justice is fused with a commitment to restoring relationship (between heaven and earth) and creating community (among men and women). The interconnections between these aspects of the significance of the cross are paradoxical and bringing them together was a costly business. However, that these things are found together in what Christians regard as the pinnacle of divine activity presents us with an inspiring challenge. Can we develop a criminal justice system in which there is a creative partnership between the punishment of wrongdoing and the (re)building of relationships?

The new community established in the light of the cross had experienced forgiveness and received, in the gift of the Holy Spirit, new moral resources. Nonetheless, this new community encountered problems. From time to time, some member would break, even flagrantly flout, the community's code of behaviour. In 1 Corinthians 5 Paul responds to reports of sexual immorality in the church at Corinth (a man sleeping with his stepmother) falling short of Christian ideals, condemned by Jewish law, and even denounced by pagans (eg Cicero).[33] In doing so Paul gives us one of the clearest examples of New Testament guidance on community action in the face of wrongdoing. Paul seeks to end the complacency of the church and stir them up to grieve over this moral failure and to take action by excluding the man in question from their fellowship. As C K Barrett observes 'Any community inculcating moral standards . . . is bound to recognise a degree beyond which transgression of its code becomes intolerable because destructive of the foundations on which the community itself rests, so that exclusion becomes necessary.'[34]

The act of exclusion is to take place when the believers 'are assembled in the name of the Lord Jesus'.[35] The whole community was to participate in an action of such solemnity and severity as the exclusion of one of its members. Paul's instruction to them is cast in perplexing language: 'hand this man over to Satan so that his body may be destroyed and his spirit saved on the day of the Lord'. The references to Satan and the body's destruction are much debated.[36] What this verse clearly demonstrates is that Paul is concerned not only with the purity of the church but also with the ultimate salvation of the erring member. The interests of the community's life are not allowed to eclipse the interests of the offender.

There is, or may be, a sequel to this episode. In 2 Corinthians 2 Paul writes of someone who has been disciplined:

> The punishment inflicted on him by the majority is sufficient for him. Now instead, you ought to forgive and comfort him, so that he will not be overwhelmed by excessive sorrow. I urge you, therefore, to reaffirm your love for him.[37]

Commentators disagree on who is in view here; it might be the incestuous man. In any event, these verses demonstrate that the community was, always or typically, to see punishment as a stage in a process in which an offender was restored to the community. The word translated 'punishment' (*epitimia*) occurs in the New Testament here only but is used in extra-biblical writings of legal penalties and suggests that 'the congregation had acted formally and judicially against the offender'.[38] The word translated 'to reaffirm' (*kyrosai*) was used to confirm a sale or ratify an appointment. 'The confirmation of love for which Paul calls, then, appears to be some formal act by the congregation, in the same way that the imposition of punishment . . . appears to have been'.[39] It may be asked, today, whether there should be 're-acceptance procedures' in our criminal justice system.

Our consideration of the New Testament may be concluded by drawing attention to the fundamental place relationships play in the Christian conception of reality. The first Christians knew from their Jewish roots that 'the Lord is one'[40] but found that they encountered God as Father, Son and Holy Spirit. The Church Fathers, in the light of the New Testament witness, developed the concept of God as Trinity, one God yet three persons in relationship. At the heart of the universe, from before time, is an everlasting community. Men and women, created by such a God, are made for relationship. Moreover, the presence within the Godhead of relationships characterized by harmony, mutuality and intimacy underpins the New Testament declaration that 'God is love'[41] and helps to explain why a Christian ethic is, *par excellence*, an ethic of love.

The Qur'an[42]

Islam means submission to God. In practice, the will of Allah to which the Muslim must submit is the law which expresses the divine will. Islamic law is enshrined in the *shari'a* (literally 'the pathway') and embraces every detail of human life. As the guide to all human action, Islam accords to its sacred law a pre-eminent role and status. There are several recognised sources of law in Islam: the Qur'an, the *sunna* (the practice of the Prophet), *qiyas* (analogy allowing the principles in the Qur'an and *sunna* to be extended to new situations) and *ijma* (the consensus of Muslim juristic scholars). In addition, customary law among pre-Islamic Arabs was a significant influence. Today, while there are Muslim fundamentalists urging a return to the *shari 'a*, in most Muslim states other than Saudi Arabia its sphere of influence in national law is largely restricted to family matters, such as matrimonial and inheritance law.

Our focus of concern, however, is the Qur'an, a text containing far less material of a legal nature than the Torah. It is not, however, silent on the subject of justice.

The rule of Allah must be delegated and the person he appoints as ruler is to rule with justice. Hence, Allah's words to David:

> David, we have made you master in the land. Rule with justice among men.[43]

Moreover, the characteristic of the believer should be to promote justice. Thus:

> The true believers, both men and women, are friends to one another. They enjoin what is just and forbid what is evil . . .[44]

The Qur'an has several words for justice but the most frequent is *'adl*:

> Literally, the word *'adl* is an abstract noun, derived from the verb *'adala*, which means: First, to straighten or to sit straight, to amend or modify; second, to run away, depart or deflect from one [wrong] path to the other [right] one; third, to be equal or equivalent, to be equal or match, or to equalize; fourth, to balance or counter-balance, to weigh, or to be in a state of equilibrium . . . The literal meaning of *'adl* in classical Arabic is thus a combination of moral and social values denoting fairness, balance, temperance and straightforwardness.[45]

While the Qur'an requires men to act with justice there is some debate within Islam as to whether Allah himself is necessarily just. A school of thinkers known as the Mu'tazila taught that God must 'act in accordance with justice and always do what was best for his creatures'.[46] However, the more accepted view is that there 'could be no necessity upon God even to do justice, and man must unquestioningly accept whatever he did'.[47] This is not so much a suggestion that Allah is unjust as the conviction that God's character and actions cannot be limited to human definitions and experiences. Under the doctrine of *mukhalafa* (difference) God is so different from his creatures that it is virtually impossible to postulate anything about him. He may describe himself as 'the Merciful' but this quality need have no connection with the human concept of mercy. The result is that 'Islam is, indeed, exceedingly rich in what Muslims believe to be divine disclosures of God's will for man, but the mystery of God himself—his person, nature and character—remain shrouded in largely negative abstractions.'[48]

Muslim communities are often tight knit and the Qur'an, while regulating family life in ways contrary to widely accepted Western views on fair treatment for women, contains principles calculated to strengthen aspects of community life. 'In many places in the Qur'an good treatment of the *Zawil Qurba* (near relations) is enjoined.'[49] Neighbours 'are deserving of fellow-feeling, affection, courtesy and fair treatment'.[50] Community and personal freedom are both valued but community is more highly prized. The 'principles of brotherhood and equality, forming the very foundation of the community of believers (*umma*)' are the ones extolled.[51]

In Islamic law the two sources from which all 'penal law is commonly derived' are 'private vengeance and punishment of crimes against religion'.[52] The first category, giving rise to laws permitting and regulating retaliation, deals with offences such as murder, manslaughter and injury. The Qur'an permits retaliation on the basis of 'a life for a life, an eye for an eye, a nose for a nose, an ear for an ear, a tooth for a tooth, and a wound for a wound' in response to homicide, or as the case may be, injury.[53]

The *wali al-dam* (literally 'avenger of blood') who is the next-of-kin has the right to demand retaliation for homicide. The Qur'an however recommends waiving retaliation, in which case the next of kin may take blood money instead or grant a full pardon.[54] Under the *shari'a* retaliation only applies to homicide committed with deliberate intent. [55] In cases of injury, the injured person has the right to demand retaliation but the Qur'an again recommends waiving retaliation in which case blood money may be required. Under the *shari'a* retaliation is 'restricted to those cases in which exact equality can be assured, eg the loss of a hand',[56] a fact which often precludes its application.

Crimes against religion are certain of the acts forbidden in the Qur'an, and these include unlawful intercourse, drinking wine, highway robbery and theft. The punishment or *hadd* is a claim of Allah and thus fixed and unalterable and takes the form, depending on the crime, of capital punishment, amputation of hand or foot or flogging. The court has no option to pursue a different course. To the Western mind the severity of the command to cut off the hand of a man or woman guilty of theft[57] is a stark example of the austerity which often characterises Islam. However, in Islamic law 'there is a strong tendency to restrict the applicability of *hadd* punishments as much as possible . . .'.[58] Such punishments are only imposed if proof of guilt has been established under extremely stringent rules of evidence.

Conclusion

Is it possible to build a measure of consensus between a 'secular' view of justice, first with that of any given faith and, secondly, with the three religions considered above? We are not in a position after so slender a discussion to address that question in any decisive sense. Contemporary religious views and practice are not synonymous with those sketched out above and the diversity of secular views has not been considered. The relationship of state and religion and the basis, scope and limits of mutual tolerance by secular and religious members of society would need to be explored.

Nonetheless, while not wishing in any way to ignore the differences between the faiths, from this chapter alone points of convergence are apparent in the three religious traditions. Some relate to theological convictions. Judaism, Christianity and Islam regard God as the ultimate source of justice. In the first two, justice is unambiguously linked to the character of God though, as we have seen, many Muslims would trace the justice which human societies should practice only as far as the commands of God. Many, however, relate to community dynamics and to some extent community values. Each faith gives rise to a community which strives to uphold shared values and, accordingly, establishes boundaries of acceptable behaviour. To maintain them, each is prepared to take action to preserve its integrity and, *in extremis*, that may involve removing an offender from the community. Each faith is willing to contemplate severity but prefers punishment with respect and restoration and/or encourages mercy. In all three, retributive justice is a crucial element. Punishment may be imposed by the community as a whole or inflicted by the aggrieved party with the approval of the community but the notion that the offender's actions deserve such a response is important to the moral legitimacy of such action. The distinctions between the religions rest, significantly, in the extent to which this principle is accompanied, adjusted, and perhaps tempered by other priorities. Despite the strong emphasis within Islam on community ties, Relational Justice has a more natural affinity with the Judaeo-Christian tradition. Relationships are seen as integral to social reality (Judaism) or ultimate reality (Christianity) in a way that makes inescapable the priority of respect for the offender and the importance of seeking his full reintegration into the life of the community.

144

Notes

1 R J Zwi Werblowsky, 'Judaism, or the Religion of Israel' in R.C Zaehner, ed, *The Concise Encyclopaedia of Living Faiths* (London: Hutchinson, 1971), p 10.

2 See eg W Eichrodt, *Theology of the Old Testament* (2 vols, Philadelphia: Westminster, 1975), I, pp 240-1.

3 Deuteronomy 16:20. The translation is drawn from M Galinski, *Pursue Justice: The Administration of Justice in Ancient Israel* (London: Nechdim Press, 1983), p 1.

4 J P Miranda, *Marx and the Bible* (London: SCM Press: 1977), p 109.

5 C J H Wright, *Living as the People of God* (Leicester: Inter-Varsity Press, 1983), p 134.

6 Psalm 85:10. Biblical quotations are drawn from the New International Version, unless otherwise stated.

7 E M Gershfield, ed, *Studies in Jewish Jurisprudence* (4 vols, New York: Hermon Press, 1971), I, p 11.

8 Deuteronomy 1:16-17.

9 Deuteronomy 25:1.

10 H J Boecker, *Law and the Administration of Justice in the Old Testament and Ancient Near East* (London: SPCK, 1980), p 37.

11 Leviticus 5:1.

12 Numbers 5:5-7.

13 Exodus 23:4-5.

14 See eg 2 Samuel 15:1-6 and 2 Chronicles 19:4-11.

15 M Galinski, *Pursue Justice*, op. cit., p 7.

16 Psalm 72:1-2.

17 Psalm 89:14.

18 See eg discussion of Exodus 21:22-27 in R de Vaux, *Ancient Israel: Its Life and its Institutions* (London: Darton, Longman & Todd, 1973). In Judaism, the *lex talionis* was early reinterpreted (though not always understood) as requiring monetary compensation commensurate with the bodily harm inflicted. See eg discussion of rabbinic debate in H H Cohn, 'The Penology of the Talmud', in H H Cohn, *Jewish Law in Ancient and Modern Isreal* (Ktav Publishing House Inc, 1971), p 72-80.

19 R de Vaux, *Ancient Israel: Its Life and its Institutions, op cit,* p 159.

20 Capital punishment was imposed for the following offences: idolatry, blasphemy, sabbath breaking (which was in effect a repudiation of the covenant), witchcraft and false prophecy, intentional homicide, rape, kidnapping, false witness in a capital case, striking or cursing a parent, adultery, bestiality/incest/homosexual intercourse, and unchastity.

21 See G J Wenham, 'Law and the Legal System', p 39 in B N Kaye, and G J Wenham, eds, *Law, Morality and the Bible* (Leicester: Inter-Varsity Press, 1978).

22 Numbers 5:7.

23 Exodus 22:1.

24 Deuteronomy 25:1-3.

25 G R Diver and J C Miles, *The Babylonian Laws* (Oxford: Clarendon Press, 1952), I, p 501 quoted in G J Wenham, 'Law and the legal system in the Old Testament', p 44, in B N Kaye, and G J Wenham, eds, *Law, Morality and the Bible, op cit.* Imprisonment was, in fact, not completely unknown in practice in ancient Israel (see eg 1 Kings 22:27; Jeremiah 32:2).

26 D J Goldberg and J D Rayner, The Jewish People: Their History and their Religion (London: Penguin, 1989), p 298.

27 Romans 3:26.

28 *Ibid.*

[29] Romans 13:4.

[30] 1 Peter 2:14.

[31] W Temple, *The Ethics of Penal Action* (London: The Clarke Hall Fellowship, 1934), p 40.

[32] Romans 3:22b-23.

[33] C K Barrett, *The First Epistle to the Corinthians* (London: A & C Black, 1971), p 123.

[34] *Ibid*, p 123.

[35] 1 Corinthians 5:4.

[36] 1 Corinthians 5:5. The former is, basically, a way of describing expulsion from the church. The latter may mean that Paul envisages removal from the secure realm of the church will lead to physical consequences; certainly one day the man will die physically though not spiritually. See eg C K Barrett, *The First Epistle to the Corinthians, op cit*, pp 124-7 and L Morris, *The First Epistle of Paul to the Corinthians* (Leicester, Inter-Varsity Press, 1985), pp 85-6.

[37] 2 Corinthians 2:6-8.

[38] C G Kruse, *The Second Epistle of Paul to the Corinthians* (Leicester: Inter-Varsity Press, Tyndale New Testament Commentaries, 1987), pp 81-2.

[39] *Ibid*, p 82.

[40] Deuteronomy 6:4.

[41] 1 John 4:8.

[42] In the transliteration of some of the arabic words in this section some letters should be accompanied by phonetic symbols which it has not been possible to reproduce in this imprint.

[43] Qur'an 38:26. The reference indicates that the quotation is from the 26th verse of the 38th *Sura* of the Qur'an. Quotations from the Qur'an are taken from *The Koran*, trans'd N J Dawood (London: Penguin, 1993).

[44] Qur'an 9:71.

[45] M Khadduri, *The Islamic Conception of Justice* (Baltimore: Johns Hopkins University Press, 1984), pp 6,8.

[46] *Ibid*, p 19.

[47] J N D Anderson, *Islam in the Modern World —A Christian Perspective* (Leicester: Apollos, 1990), p 19.

[48] J N D Anderson, *God's Law and God's Love: An Essay in Comparative Religion* (London: Collins, 1980), p 104.

[49] S Abul A'la Maududi, *Islamic Way of Life*, tr K Ahmad (Nairobi: The Islamic Foundation, 1978), p 54.

[50] *Ibid*, p 55.

[51] M Khadduri, *The Islamic Conception of Justice, op cit*, p 143.

[52] J Schacht, *An Introduction to Islamic Law* (Oxford: Clarendon Press, 1964), p 175.

[53] Qur'an 2:178.

[54] Qur'an 2:178, 5:49. See J Schacht, *An Introduction to Islamic Law, op cit*, pp 181-7 for the expression of these principles under the *shari a*.

[55] J Schacht, *An Introduction to Islamic law, op. cit.*, p. 181.

[56] *Ibid*, p 185.

[57] Qur'an 5:38.

[58] J Schacht, *An Introduction to Islamic Law, op cit*, p 187.

CHAPTER 12

Repairing the Breach: A Personal Motivation

Peter Walker

Terry was a petty burglar who had served several short prison sentences. Then one theft went horribly wrong and left a man dead. Terry was convicted and sentenced to life imprisonment. He could not come to terms with his sentence, he could not cope with the prospect of long-term prison life and he took out his aggression on prison staff and other inmates.

Terry spent time in some 20 prisons, continually being moved on until he eventually ended up in a really 'tough' prison. There he responded with yet more aggression and with threats to staff which resulted in injuries.

A senior prison officer offered to take Terry to the boxing ring during a lunchtime and invited him to fight out his aggression with him. Terry agreed. They met again on another lunchtime. Eventually a friendship built up between the two men. Terry began to understand himself better and to recognise his own feelings. Thereafter he became aware of the feelings of those around him. Changes started to take place in his life.

It is a story which reminds us of the power of human relationships to change people both for ill and for good. No man—or woman—is an island; each of us is a piece of the continent and connected to others, whether by virtue of blood choice or circumstance. Good relationships can bring about positive change through care and encouragement. Destructive relationships, such as those where there is no trust, only fear of abuse or rejection, damage people deeply.

Relationships are a reforming dynamic. But what makes a good relationship? What puts a wrong relationship right? These are questions which I will explore in this chapter from my experiences as someone involved in an organization supporting, on a day-to-day basis, individuals caught up in crime and its consequences.

Broken relationships
Broken relationships are at the heart of every crime. This is obvious in cases of physical assaults, many of which involve people well known to each other, but it is perhaps not so obvious in cases such as tax evasion or

shoplifting. Yet these crimes involve a serious breakdown of trust and ultimately result in the rest of the community having to bear the costs of extra policing and security. In this sense, all of us become victims of crime.

Crime erodes that mutual respect which is at the root of a 'good' relationship. This is surely one reason why so much public and political rhetoric about tackling crime seems to imply a view that the criminal, by offending against society's laws has abrogated his or her own right to be treated with respect. I disagree with those views—as I hope to make clear in this chapter.

To view crime primarily in terms of broken relationships between people and only secondly as an offence against society's laws gives a radically different perspective on offending and on the punishment of offending behaviour.

Offenders themselves often make a great effort to deny that their victims are human beings. A burglar may disregard the consequences of a crime believing that 'the victim can always claim the loss back from the insurance' and by refusing to consider the emotional and psychological damage that may have been caused.

A 19-year-old who claims to have carried out many hundreds of burglaries confessed that, on entering a house, if there were pictures of the family on the wall or standing on the mantelpiece, he would deliberately turn them around—or lay them down—so that he did not have to see the faces of the people he was stealing from. In a bizarre way, he recognised that he was creating victims, but he tried to avoid facing up to the full realisation of his actions against these people.

Relational Justice sees the relationship between victim and offender as a pivotal one—and the argument is that the repairing of this relationship should be a central goal of the criminal justice system. Relational Justice also recognises that broken or dysfunctional relationships, particularly within close family, can contribute towards an anti-social tendency in young people.

It is obvious that the relational thesis goes far beyond criminal justice issues. It exposes those tensions which lie at the heart of all human relationships: the conflict between putting the interests of others—or of oneself—first. Putting 'right' a broken relationship whether as a result of a criminal—or simply of a selfish—act will involve one or both parties having to become less self-centred. It is this change of heart which our criminal justice system should aim to facilitate by its procedures and outcomes. At the very least, it should not form a hindrance to moral change.

Hope for change

Hope was the last to emerge from Pandora's box. Ostensibly, our criminal justice system is founded on the hope that those who are dealt with under its processes will change their behaviour. Words like 'reform' and 'correction' have always been a part of penal vocabulary. Indeed, in the USA, prisons are still referred to as 'correctional institutions'. If hope for change is lost, the penal system risks collapsing under the weight of cynicism and despair. Without hope, only incapacitation and the tragic waste caused by the warehousing of human lives is left

The probation service is founded on the belief that there is hope for change. Although we hold some 50,000 men and women in the prisons of England and Wales, around a quarter of a million more offenders a year in this country are dealt with by the probation service and never see, nor need to see, the inside of a prison.

The task of a probation officer was always understood to be overtly relational, namely, 'to advise, assist and befriend' the probationer. The hope is that the relationship which develops between the probation officer and the offender will put right what other relationships in the offender's past history served to put wrong, perhaps by rebuilding self-esteem or simply by opening new doors to a law-abiding life. The onus in any probation order is upon the offender to choose to change, to respond to the trust placed in him or her to keep within the restrictions of the order. An offender's willingness to respond in a trustworthy manner and to respect an authority figure (perhaps for the first time) will depend largely on the nature of the relationship between the offender and the probation officer.

One of the classic teaching books on probation *The Casework Relationship*[1] saw the relationship between the probation officer and the offender/client as 'the soul of social casework' and identified the ground rules which should govern how the relationship ought to operate: recognition of the uniqueness of each individual case; acceptance; a non-judgmental attitude; confidentiality; permission to express feelings; controlled emotional involvement by the probation officer; and responsibility for decision-making by the probationer. These are the ingredients of a constructive relationship which has the potential to be a dynamic for change.

Dick was on probation for burglary and car theft. He was intelligent and could have done well at school but rebelled, particularly against his ineffective father who spent long hours running an unsuccessful business.

Dick had been out of work since leaving school without any qualifications. He hung around all day, often at home bullying his mother and demanding money from her. He resented probation but kept his appointments with the worst possible grace. The probation officer insisted on exact compliance with his instructions, meeting Dick's rudeness by continuing to show concern for his progress and expressing interest in anything positive that Dick did. This stalemate continued for months.

The turning point came when Dick acquired an old motor-cycle. The probation officer happened to be visiting one day when Dick had reached breaking point in the frustration of trying, yet again, to make it go. The officer went back to his car and got out some tools and together they worked for an hour on the engine which finally started.

After this Dick's attitude changed. He began to share his frustrations about his life and his mixed feelings of hurt and contempt for his parents and younger brother. He was able to respond to the probation officer's suggestion of trying a 'return to study' course at the local college and by the end of the probation order was well on his way to achieving qualifications on which to base a future career.

Probation orders are given to those offenders whom the courts believe could change if given the opportunity to address their behaviour with the support of a probation officer. It is this opportunity which opens the door to change—as trust is built up and understanding grows.

The hope therefore is that the criminal justice system will be there for the likes of Dick and Terry—who was mentioned at the beginning of this chapter—in the form of people who care enough to accept offenders as people and who will try to understand and not merely condemn. If an offender can build one such relationship of mutual trust, perhaps for the first time, it becomes possible to believe that the same can happen in other circumstances—maybe on a training scheme, in a job or even in a personal relationship or marriage. A supportive relationship can rebuild self-respect and an ability to accept other people in the 'give and take' of everyday life.

Sentencing someone to imprisonment, in contrast to making a probation order, may reflect a lack of faith in the ability or willingness of the offender to change. After all, prisons are not designed, primarily, to be therapeutic. Nor do prison regimes effectively address the underlying relational issues which might have led to a crime.

Potential for change

The belief that individuals have the capacity to change for the better is a major motivating factor behind the work of most of the people who I meet day by day and who work in the Prison Service, in probation and in the many voluntary agencies concerned for offenders, victims and their respective families.

The motivation behind the work of Prison Fellowship, a Christian ministry to prisoners, ex-prisoners and their families is that there is potential for change even in the most hardened offenders. Our logo is a bent reed. The prophet Isaiah says of God 'a bruised reed will not break' (Isaiah 42 v 3). This verse speaks of a God who promises to restore those who have made a mess of their lives, if they will turn to him. This love is demonstrated in practical ways through the concern and care shown by volunteers towards prisoners, ex-prisoners and their families.

The Prison Service has long recognised that there is a spiritual dimension to the 'reforming' process. The presence of chaplains at every prison establishment is a source of considerable support and encouragement to those prisoners seeking to change and to recognise that they need help. One of the more revealing findings of the survey of prisoners' attitudes conducted by Prison Fellowship and the Jubilee Policy Group[2] was the value many inmates placed on being able to talk to a prison chaplain. Chaplains came higher up the list of preferences than probation officers or social workers, prison officers or fellow inmates. More poignantly, the survey found that 38 per cent of male prisoners and 21 per cent of female prisoners had no-one who they felt they could really talk to about their situation inside the prison—with similar proportions saying that there was no-one outside prison to whom they could talk to either. Believing in the potential for change means a preparedness to get involved in offenders' lives, however chaotic or seemingly hopeless. It could also mean getting involved in their network of relationships and supporting those offending people who are struggling to keep afloat while their spouse, partner or parent is in prison.

Acting as a 'go-between' with those on the outside is an important aspect of the work of Prison Fellowship which operates among other schemes a project called Angel Tree at Christmas time. This scheme helps prisoners provide Christmas gifts to their children, as if the presents were coming from the inmates themselves, helping them to do something they cannot do by themselves. This is a simple but powerful gesture of caring which has helped a number of prisoners to keep in touch with their children while at the same time demonstrating to prisoners and their families that someone understands their situation.

Power for change

Believing in the potential for change does not mean being naive about the difficulties and obstacles which must be overcome. For a teenager with an abusive father, who was thrown out onto the streets at 16 years of age with poor mental health and a subsequent alcohol problem, it is not altogether surprising that frequent periods in prison did not result in a changed lifestyle for Eddie. However, Eddie, now in his fifties, has a sucessful window cleaning round and people who know him will say that he is a changed man. On the point of being released from another prison spell, Eddie 'prayed to go straight, for love and affection, for a roof over my head'. Shortly after discharge, he had a dramatic spiritual experience which convinced him of God's existence and love for him. A couple then took him into their home and he went with them to the church they attended. Although Eddie stopped drinking and began to take more pride in himself, he still continued to have crises, not least involving Social Services and the Department of Social Security.

Eddie's story is remarkble—but sadly, there are many more tales which do not have the same hopeful message. Nevertheless, Eddie's experience is a reminder than no-one's situation is irredeemable—because no-one is beyond the reach of God or of his followers on Earth. It is this belief that continues to motivate my work with Prison Fellowship. I know that I too can be a channel of that power for change!

Relationships—Vertical and horizontal
Through my work in prisons, I have seen the capacity of spiritual change to affect an individual's whole behaviour and outlook on life.

Jewish and Christian traditions have always acknowledged that faith is to be expressed in terms of relationships: both the 'horizontal' relationship between one person and another, and the 'vertical' relationship between an individual and God. It is central to both the Christian and Jewish faiths that it is the Creator God who longs to have a relationship with his creation and takes the initiative himself. So, Christians believe that when self-centredness and pride separated humankind from God, he sought a way of 'repairing the breach' through the life, death and resurrection of his Son, Jesus Christ. For in his love for us, God entered our world in the person of his Son. He identified himself in his life and death with all our hopes and fears. He took on himself our sin, guilt, our death in our place, in order that we might be forgiven and enjoy an open 'vertical' relationship with God.

Gospel accounts of Jesus' life on Earth exemplify ideal vertical and horizontal relationships. His life was lived out by showing complete obedience to and dependence upon his Father in Heaven and in his compassion for all those who came to him in need—especially the poor and the social outcast.

It is in receiving this forgiveness, in repentance and faith, that a renewed vertical relationship with God begins. It has been my experience, that when this vertical relationship with God begins, a new dimension to life opens up, and that other changes on the horizontal level also start to take effect.

Craig was a hardened criminal. He cared nothing for his victims or the system which had imprisoned him—and this was evident on many occasions. In the words of the television programme 'Porridge', Craig saw imprisonment as an occupational hazard. Yet like many offenders he had tried to 'go straight'. He had even got married to see if having some responsibility would help. But to no avail. He did not possess the wherewithal, within himself, to make the change.

After receiving a particularly harsh sentence, Craig was at a low personal ebb. In his Manchester prison cell, alone and in desperation he called out to a God for help. He sensed a peace within himself unlike anything he had felt before, and a sorrow for all of those people that he had hurt. In the morning Craig asked to see a member of the prison service chaplaincy team. The chaplain prayed with Craig and helped him to understand the changes that were taking place in his attitudes.

Today Craig works for an organisation which helps prisoners on release to reintegrate into the community—thereby giving them strength to form relationships.

Potential for reconciliation

Much of this chapter has centred on the offender. However, right relationships require the involvement of the other parties involved in a crime: especially the victim and the wider community.

My parents-in-law were burgled some six years ago, whilst they were away from home. They returned to find a window broken and various items stolen, including the video recorder, ornaments and jewellery. Insurance fully covered the monetary value of the stolen items—none, individually speaking, of any great financial worth. However, the real damage has not been a financial one. What has been affected quite severely is their fear of being away from home, 'in case the burglar returns'. This 'low scale property crime' has had wider repercussions, not only on two ordinary people in their seventies, but also on their children and grandchildren, who now see less of them because they fear being away from home and becoming victims again.

The criminal justice system focuses almost entirely on the offender and on achieving retribution for the crime committed. In this process, the needs of the victims are rarely, if ever, addressed. Bringing victims of crime and offenders together is one way which could provide an opportunity for reconciliation, for reparation or for some form of compensation or apology to be extended. This said, there is a recognition through the parole system that if an offender shows remorse for the harm he or she caused to the victim, it is a sign of coming to terms with the offence and the starting point for new patterns of behaviour. Yet how often are offenders seriously challenged to face up to the full impact of their actions viz-a-viz their victims?

As has been detailed by Nicola Baker in *Chapter 5* when dealing with victim/offender mediation, bringing victims and offenders together can—in appropriate cases—bring about real change in an offender's attitudes. It can also enable victims to come to terms with what happened, allay certain fears and perhaps to receive compensation material or psychological—as a means of repairing the breach of trust created by the offence.

In one case, a traffic policeman was blinded in a road accident which occured whilst he was pursuing a young car thief. The offender was caught, charged and sentenced to a term in prison. After several months spent recovering (although still not able to see), the policeman asked to meet the offender so as to explain to him, without any bitterness, the devastating impact the crime had had upon his life, family and career. The offender agreed to the interview which took place in a room within the prison.

Until then, the offender had no idea of the horrific injuries that the policeman had incurred. To him his offence had been to 'joy ride' in a stolen car. He listened in silence as the policeman related what had happened There was no bitterness, no sense of revenge, just a statement of the facts. The offender was clearly very moved, for when given the opportunity to speak, he found no words to respond to what he had just heard. After a further few minutes the offender made an attempt to express his sorrow at what he had caused to happen, but he could no longer stand the pressure of seeing his victim and left the room very disturbed.

Maybe for this young man the encounter with his victim and the understanding of the impact of the crime will have some deterrent effect. For the victim, he at least had the opportunity to explain the devastating consequences of the crime to the one who had been the direct cause of them.

It was Jesus who, through the parable of the Good Samaritan, established the role model for the work of victim support schemes. The story goes that a man was travelling along a notorious road and was set upon by robbers. Later, three people came along the same route. The first two were leaders of the 'church', a priest and then a Levite. Both of these saw the victim but passed by on the other side of the road. The third person was a man from Samaria, a despised foreigner. He stopped to help the victim, offering first aid and then helping him to a hostel where he could recover. The Samaritan paid the hostel and was prepared to meet any extra bills the next time he was passing He put the needs of the victim higher than a concern for social or racial conventions, or his busy schedule of commitments. Christ's words to his hearers, and to us today were 'go and do likewise' (Luke 10 v 37)

The heart of Relational Justice

At the heart of Relational Justice is an understanding that human relationships are profoundly significant and offer the potential for a powerful dynamic for change, both for good or ill. If we as a society are concerned about crime and about its damaging impact on relationships, direct and indirect then our response to crime will need to reflect a concern for mending and repairing that damage.

Many of us who work with those caught up in the consequences of crime want to see our justice system operating as an instrument for achieving repair. In many places this is happening where men and women who work in and alongside the system are committed to treating offenders, victims and their respective families and friends with due respect, courtesy and compassion. Relational Justice offers all of use a challenge to look again at how our justice system actually impacts on people's lives.

I warmly welcome Relational Justice because I believe it brings a much-needed ray of hope into the system at a critical time. I fully endorse its basic premise that people, even the most unlikely people, can change if given the opportunity to build and sustain constructive relationships. I believe that the justice process should create more space for this to happen.

Notes

1 Fr Felix Biestek S J, The Casework Relationship (London, 1957)
2 Jubilee Policy Group, *Relational Justice: A new approach to penal reform*, Interim Report 1991/2 (Cambridge, Jubilee Policy Group, 1992)

Part IV

Policy Implications

13 Relational Justice: A Dynamic for Reform
David Faulkner

CHAPTER 13

Relational Justice:
A Dynamic for Reform

David Faulkner

Previous chapters in this volume have approached the problems of crime, injustice and social instability from a variety of personal and professional backgrounds, and from different philosophical perspectives. What all the various contributors have in common is that they see those problems as resulting from failures in relationships—between individuals, between individuals and institutions, and between individuals and their communities. They have sought remedies which would restore, repair or re-create those relationships. Some contributors have provided a general analysis; others have put forward specific proposals. Not all contributors would necessarily agree with all the proposals which have been put forward or all the views which have been expressed, and proposals which might follow naturally from one contributor's analysis might not be supported by another. Relational Justice is not offered as a paradigm or a comprehensive test of all public policy, but relational values can provide an important and often new perspective, an inter-connected set of ideas which can help to illuminate issues, indicate the directions in which future policies might lead, and provide a new dynamic for reform. They have a much wider application than issues of crime and criminal justice, as Michael Schluter explains in *Chapter 1*.

A new debate
This chapter attempts to draw from those contributions, and to some extent from the writer's own experience, a set of recommendations which can be offered to those in suitable positions of authority as a means of developing the theme of Relational Justice and of putting it into practical effect. Positions of authority may for this purpose be in central government or in Parliament; or in local authorities, statutory services, practising professions, commercial organizations and voluntary bodies. The concept of Relational Justice is related to the concepts of citizenship, support for communities, social responsibility and civil society, all of which are now being explored from different points in the political spectrum. Many of

them can be understood in different ways, and the discussion can often point towards different conclusions. But it is interesting and very significant that concern about the social and moral fabric of society, and about the problems of crime and the humiliation, indignity, isolation and the lack of confidence in existing institutions and procedures which are associated with it, has led to a revival of interest in principles. For a long time—perhaps for too long—the country's decision-makers have been impatient or suspicious of intellectual analysis and have preferred to concentrate on immediate problems and practical solutions. Even so, intellectual discourse should always suggest practical outcomes, and these are what the present chapter tries to offer.

Contrasting views of policy and organization

It is important to recognise the very real differences in attitude, outlook and approach which lie behind the debate as it has been conducted so far. They may reflect different political backgrounds or different philosophical positions, eg the contrast between the classical views of free will and determinism, and the different views of justice which Jonathan Burnside examines in *Chapter 3*. They may reflect different kinds of personal or professional experience. They certainly reflect different views of human behaviour and personal motivation.

Many current policies—in the field of criminal justice but also social and economic policies more generally—reflect a view of human life and human behaviour which emphasises personal freedom and individual responsibility, but which disregards the influence of situations and circumstances. It is associated with the notion of a 'deserving' majority who are self-reliant and law-abiding and who should be entitled to benefit themselves and those around them without interference from others; and an undeserving, feckless, welfare-dependent and potentially criminal minority—or under-class—from whom they need to be protected.

Human behaviour is thought to be motivated mainly by a desire for material gain or by fear of punishment or disgrace: there is not much interest in, or respect for, notions of social justice or public duty or service. Crime is to be prevented by efficiency of detection, certainty of conviction and severity of punishment, including the incapacitating effect of imprisonment. | Justice is seen as an instrument of social control for protecting the innocent from the guilty or the deserving from the undeserving, and it can be measured by its effectiveness in achieving that purpose.| Within organizations, including those concerned with criminal justice, this view has its counterpart in an approach to management which emphasises material rewards, typically in: performance pay; the discipline of competition and the threat of dismissal; and a top-down structure of output measures and performance indicators. Not much is made of such notions as equity, personal loyalty or mutual trust.

The contrasting view recognises the capacity of individuals to change—to improve if they are given guidance, help and encouragement; to be damaged if they are abused or humiliated. It emphasises respect for human dignity and personal identity. It looks more towards putting things right for the future and to making things whole than to punishing the past (although the latter may sometimes be part of the former). The criminal justice process is not by itself expected to do much to reduce crime or mitigate its effects, and the means of doing so have to be sought elsewhere. Authority will not be respected if it is simply imposed: it has to be accountable and legitimate, and respect has to be earned and justified. Respect for the law and consideration for others are learned by explanation, discussion, experience and example. Within organizations, the emphasis is on a participative style of management, on teams as well as individuals, on the quality of relations within the organization and outside of it, and on improving and recognising performance rather than punishing failure. An organization's internal style must match the function it has to perform: if staff in services like the police or the court, probation and prison services do not feel respected themselves they will not easily show respect for others, or receive it in return.

Andrew Coyle develops this point in relation to the Prison Service in *Chapter 10.*

Citizenship and communities
Similar differences of view can be found in debates about citizenship and communities. On one view, a person has to 'qualify' for citizenship or membership of a community, and the benefits are confined to those who conform to certain standards or who can afford to buy them. Those who take this view are likely to favour the extension of patrolled and defended space in shopping precincts or residential estates; the proposed criminalisation of squatters and travellers; the continued disqualification of victims from compensation for criminal injuries on the grounds of their own unrelated criminal convictions; and the introduction of a national identity card. Offenders are seen as having forfeited their right to citizenship and membership of their communities. There is little interest in notions of citizenship which are associated with the possession of inalienable or enforceable rights.

This 'exclusive' view of citizenship can be contrasted with an 'inclusive' view in which a person's citizenship and entitlement to consideration and respect are never entirely lost and communities have obligations to their members as well as vice versa. There is an emphasis on equal opportunities and the protection of minorities, and interest in a Bill of Rights and a written constitution. Communities must acknowledge and respect diversity and plurality. Judgments in court should be based on what a person has done, and not on who or what they are. Offenders should not be denied access to the ordinary benefits of citizenship, or be excluded from their communities, except to the extent that such denial is an inevitable consequence of the decision of a court, taken after a full legal process. Imprisonment should be avoided so far as possible.

Relational Justice —an extra dimension

None of these views can be regarded as wholly 'right' or wholly 'wrong' in the sense that they must always, or never, prevail whatever the circumstances. Most people are likely to take an eclectic view of the practical conclusions which can be drawn from them. Relational Justice can, however, add an important extra dimension to the argument. It will usually suggest the second rather than the first of each of the pairs of views set out in the previous four paragraphs, but it will also acknowledge—and try to respond to—the pressure for difficult children to be excluded from school; the resentment among local people when a well-known trouble-maker is seen out and about immediately after a conviction in court; the victim's sense of being let down when the often painful ordeal of giving evidence does not result in the defendant's conviction or what is thought to be an adequate sentence; and the apprehension which the victim of a serious offence may feel when the offender is released from prison. Relational Justice will nevertheless acknowledge that offenders are not a separate class, to be thought about in a different way to other people, and that many offenders have previously been victims and vice versa. As Roger Shaw points out in *Chapter 9*, an offender's punishment may involve an even more severe punishment for his or her innocent family. Relational Justice will also recognise that the formal structures of local authorities, courts, statutory services and voluntary organizations need to be complemented by informal networks to provide help and support for those in difficulty, including the victims of crime, those who are vulnerable or disadvantaged, and offenders themselves or those at risk of offending. Examples are: understanding and co-operative neighbours; sympathetic teachers and employers; concerned landlords and landladies; helpful staff in shops, cafes, pubs, and in the Post Office or on public transport; and families themselves.

Courtesy, dignity and respect

The first of this chapter's recommendations is general and wide ranging, but it is also of immense practical significance. It is simply that all those involved in the criminal justice process should treat people with whom they come into contact—in whatever situation or capacity—with courtesy, dignity and respect. This may seem obvious, but it is all too easily overlooked in practice. It requires people to be prepared to stop and listen, to answer questions and hear arguments or complaints, and to give reasons for decisions in terms which will help people who are affected to understand and respect decisions even if they go against them. It involves sensitivity to race, gender and culture. It seeks to preserve a sense of being valued as a human being, and of some hope for the future, even if the person has done something dreadfully wrong.[1] It avoids the deliberate or unintended humiliation of one person by another. It tries to respond not only to situations as they present themselves, but also to look for the unspoken signs that a person may need an explanation or reassurance, and to remember those who may be worrying unnoticed or unseen. It applies between colleagues in the same service or occupation and to the culture which they communicate to one another; between colleagues in different services or occupations; between those in authority and suspects and offenders; and in all situations involving victims. There are all kinds of reasons why these standards can be neglected. They include financial or management pressure, lack of confidence, lack of information, exhaustion, fear of losing face, or repugnance for what someone has done or is thought to have done. Such standards are often implicit in the mission statement or in the statement of purpose of the service concerned; they are to some extent embodied or implicit in the *Victim's Charter*[2] and in the *Citizen's Charter*[3] and the charters associated with it. They need to be reinforced by measures of performance, where this is practicable, and by training and example so that they become firmly embedded in the culture and professional outlook of the services concerned. Work on the development of the *Citizen's Charter* should be extended to cover these wider aspects of the relationships involved in the delivery of public services in the criminal justice field.

Recognition of the victim

This first recommendation has special significance in relation to the victims of crime and to the families of victims. It is only in the last 15 years or so that victims of crime have been recognised as having any special interest in the cases in which they are involved or as needing any special understanding or support. A lot has been achieved during that period, most of it through the efforts of Victim Support and other voluntary organisations.[4] The *Victim's Charter* sets out much of what is implied for victims by the previous recommendation. There is still some way to go before it is fully incorporated in the day-to-day practice of all the services which may be involved with victims, but the principles are clear.

Much less clear are the forms of compensation or reparation, and recognition more generally, to which victims should be entitled from society as a whole; and the extent to which they should have a formal role in the criminal justice process which goes beyond an entitlement to be given explanations and information and to be treated with sympathy and respect.

Compensation, particularly financial compensation, was the subject of a report by an independent working party, set up by Victim Support, which was published at the end of 1993.[5] It received comparatively little attention, having been overshadowed by the dispute over the changes which the government was making to its own Criminal Injuries Compensation Scheme—an important, but much more narrow issue.

The working party said that:

> Arguments based on human dignity, on equity (including the obligation to make public expenditure towards the victim not totally disproportionate to what is spent on the apprehension, conviction and punishment of the offender), on social justice (the responsibility of society to or for its least fortunate members), and on the basic human right to some form of recognition and reparation, seemed to us to amount to an unanswerable case for providing compensation. A civilised society denounces violence and seeks to protect the innocent against the guilty and, to the extent that it can do so, it will be more stable and confident than one which does not.

It concluded that the purpose of state compensation for victims could be expressed as:

> . . . to recognise on behalf of society the experience which victims of crime have suffered; and to help the victim to recover from it and to live as normal a life as is possible in the circumstances.

It recognised, however, that:

> Compensation is only one means of helping the victim back to normal life. Provision for compensation in no way reduces the obligation of government to support the specialised agencies which exist for this purpose, including Victim Support, which may be able to contribute more to the victim's recovery and well-being than any financial compensation. The government, and the community as a whole, has a similar duty to recognise, and to take account of, the suffering which victims have experienced.

Although financial compensation is extremely important to victims, it is very unlikely to cover the whole loss or injury—psychological and material—suffered by many victims. Here Relational Justice will point to the inadequacy of most financial compensation schemes to fully meet victim's needs and would advocate extending the use of reparation in addition to establishing a more equitable and coherent policy for the payment of compensation to crime victims.

The Victim Support working party made a number of recommendations for giving practical effect to this approach, the effect of which would be to ensure adequate and prompt access to compensation payments. They are all within the spirit of Relational Justice:

> Victims of violent crime should receive compensation awards for pain, suffering and loss of amenity. Entitlement should extend not only to those who have been the victim of a crime of violence, but also to those who have experienced psychological injury as a result of other offences, such as domestic burglary or those having a racial aspect. Additional payments should be available where the physical or psychological effects of the injury persist over a long period which could not have been foreseen . . .

> Financial support should also be available, under separate arrangements and on a basis of need, to victims of property crime who suffer serious hardship. Payments should again be made by the Department of Social Security; they should be treated as grants and not recovered as loans . . .

> There should be suitable provision for victims to receive assistance and support in preparing their claims, and where necessary advice, including legal advice. There should be a system of appeals, to the agency in the first instance and then to an independent authority, with ultimate access to the courts on points of law or for judicial review.

The government and other relevant organisations should give serious attention to these recommendations, and should draw up a programme for putting them into effect.

The victim's role in the criminal justice process is part of a wider question of the implications of Relational Justice for the role of the courts, the Crown Prosecution Service and the practising legal profession. It is dealt with later in this chapter.

Services, courts and the professions
Within the criminal justice system itself, the implications of Relational Justice are relatively straightforward for the Prison Service and to some extent for the Probation Service; more complicated for the police; and more complicated still for the courts and those who practise in them.

Justice in prisons
For the Prison Service, most of the work has been done by Lord Woolf and Judge Stephen Tumim in their report on the prison disturbances which took place in April 1990.[6] The government has accepted most of their recommendations in its White Paper *Custody, Care and Justice* published

in 1992.[7] The task is less to develop fresh ideas than to sustain the momentum, and avoid distractions, in carrying forward the recommendations in that report. Their effect, if fully implemented, would be to:

- abolish the most degrading aspects of prison life especially the practice of 'slopping out'— and overcrowding;
- improve standards of fairness and justice both through formal procedures such as the appointment of an independent Complaints Adjudicator, and through the development of 'compacts' or 'contracts' with prisoners and closer and more systematic links with the prisoners' own communities, including 'community prisons';
- provide for an enhanced and more 'relational' role for prison officers.

The twelve main recommendations contained in the Woolf Report are set out in the appendix to this chapter. Again, they are all in the spirit of Relational Justice, and they match Andrew Coyle's analysis in *Chapter 10*. Further recommendations in the same spirit could include allowing male prisoners to choose their own clothes (women are already allowed to do so), and a less formal style of dress for prison officers. A longer term aim should be to reduce the loss of personal dignity which is involved in the present arrangements regarding visits and personal possessions, and to overcome the problems of security which would be regarded as obstructing such a development at present.

Probation and communities
Recommendations for the probation service ought in principle to be equally straightforward. Relationships is a subject where the probation service believes that it has distinctive skills and special expertise, and the concept of Relational Justice is thus one with which members of the service will identify—and towards which they are likely to feel sympathetic. Part of the task will be for that service to resist temptations or pressures, eg to introduce an element of deliberate humiliation into community sentences or the electronic monitoring of curfew orders; or to remove the present requirement whereby offenders must consent to the terms of orders placing them under the supervision of that service. The importance of this consent is not to comply with the requirements of the European Convention on Human Rights as they affect forced labour, but to give the order itself the legitimacy and the moral authority which comes from the offender's

acceptance of its terms. It is an important part of Relational Justice, and not a matter to be treated as an awkward technicality.

However, the task is not simply one of resisting change. The probation service is coming under increasing pressure to show that it can deliver results, in terms of improvements in the behaviour of offenders; and ultimately of lower levels of crime and increased public safety and confidence. The means by which it is doing so include greater emphasis on *confronting* offending behaviour and *holding offenders to account*, and greater sensitivity to the situations and feelings of victims.[8] The service may also need to consider a more authoritarian role for probation staff in requiring high standards of behaviour from those under their supervision, but in a context which emphasises the importance of its own accountability and legitimacy.[9] The courts should impose community sentences rather than sentences of imprisonment wherever it is possible to do so. The probation service will need to work with a widening network of other organisations which will perform particular functions or provide particular services, whether under contract or otherwise.

The probation service will also need support from the informal networks of concerned citizens of the kind already mentioned in this chapter—a point which Christopher Compston makes in *Chapter 6*. The government should consider how such networks can most effectively be encouraged and sustained.

The situation will be complicated, demanding and potentially precarious. Relationships of the kind which it demands may not be easy to sustain under the pressures of financial stringency, managerial accountability and possibly punitive public opinion which the service may have to face for the foreseeable future. The concept of Relational Justice will fully endorse the developments and the relationships which are required: it can set the parameters within which the developments could take place, and provide the energy to sustain them in the face of conflict and difficulty.

The objects of policing

The situation regarding the police is more complex. Since the earliest days of the Metropolitan Police, the service has had two main tasks—to prevent crime, and to detect and arrest offenders. The two are not the same, and they may on occasions be in conflict. The distinction and possible conflict were recognised by Sir Richard Mayne and Colonel Rowan, the first Commissioners of the Metropolitan Police, when they said in 1829:

> The primary object of an efficient police is the prevention of crime; the next that of detection and punishment of offenders if crime is committed. To these

ends, all the efforts of the police should be directed. The protection of life and property, the preservation of public tranquility, and the absence of crime, will alone prove whether those efforts have been successful, and whether the objects for which the police were appointed have been attained.

They later said that:

> It should be understood, at the outset, that the principal object to be attained is 'the prevention of crime'. To this great end every effort of the police should be directed.

Over the years, the task of 'catching villains', and if possible 'locking them up', came to assume greater importance in the culture of the police. The comparative neglect of the preventive role, and the emphasis on technology and equipment rather than personal contact, led to the unintended development of police methods which were sometimes seen as arbitrary, discriminatory, insensitive and unjust. The urban riots of the early 1980s, the criticism of police methods which led to the Police and Criminal Evidence Act 1984, and the notorious miscarriages of justice which came to light in the late 1980s, all led to a reappraisal of police methods and the role of the police service. New initiatives included the development of community policing with its emphasis on sensitivity to the situation and the feelings of all those with whom the police come into contact, and especially of victims; more rigorous standards of investigation and interrogation; the use of cautioning rather than prosecution in suitable cases; and a new initiative to promote quality of service. The police no longer saw themselves as a 'thin blue line', fighting a 'war' against an 'enemy' which had to be humiliated and defeated.

The situation is now confused and uncertain.[10] The Police and Magistrates' Court Act 1994 and the Criminal Justice and Public Order Act 1994 create new structures and give new powers to the Secretary of State and to the police themselves. Many of the provisions of these two statutes are controversial—the new custodial sentences for children, the new criminal offences relating to demonstrators, squatters and travellers, the inferences to be drawn from a suspect's refusal to answer police questions. A government review of police functions is taking place. The political emphasis is now strongly on detection and arrest, and on certainty of conviction and severity of punishment, rather than the prevention of crime or community relations. The language of warfare has returned to political debate.

It is at present difficult to see what effect the new legislation, or the outcome of the Home Office review, will have in practice. The test will be in the way in which they are implemented—whether it is in a spirit of defending the 'deserving' or 'law-abiding' members of society against an 'undeserving' or criminal class which threatens their property and personal safety; or in a spirit of preventing crime, resolving conflicts, promoting relationships, and protecting the community as a whole. As for the probation service, Relational Justice can set the parameters and provide the energy to sustain professional standards and support professional leadership. The reforms should be implemented, and the new powers should be exercised, in a spirit which acknowledges the relational aspects of all police work, and the importance of the service's role in preventing crime and supporting communities as well as its role in law enforcement.

The courts and those who practise in them

The situation regarding the courts, the Crown Prosecution Service and the practising legal profession is more complicated still. At one level the concept of Relational Justice should clearly apply to the organization of court business. Christopher Compston deals with this aspect in *Chapter 6*. Parties, witnesses and victims should all be treated with consideration and respect. Information, help and advice should be readily available. Witnesses should not be kept waiting for long periods. Waiting areas should be clean and comfortable. Victims and defendants, and prosecution and defence witnesses, should not have to meet face-to-face. Court decisions should be explained to those affected by them in language which they can understand and in terms which they can respect. The proceedings should not take place 'over the heads' of those involved in the events which are at issue, or have the appearance of an elaborate performance or ritual which has no connection with reality as they understand it. All this is understood quite well in theory, but there is sometimes a long way to go before it is applied in practice.

There are however several ways in which the organization of the courts might be made more accessible and relational, and more locally accountable. Christopher Compston suggests that courts should have a stronger local identity, with more local involvement and public discussion. The government, and the courts themselves, should give serious consideration to the suggestions he has made. The *Courts Charter* should be strengthened to take them into account.

Relational and procedural justice

Far more difficult is the application of Relational Justice to the proceedings themselves—to rules of evidence, the burden of proof, techniques of examination and cross-examination, the principles of sentencing, the balance between the lawyer's duty to the client and his or her wider duty to the public, the role of the victim, the adversarial system in general. On one view, it could be claimed that the whole point of the adversarial system is that it should not be relational—that in respect of the verdict the issue is whether the defendant is guilty of the offence according to the accepted standards of proof; and that in respect of the sentence it is commensurate with the seriousness of the offence and in some instances the need to protect the public. These principles are arguably more important than the situation and feelings of the victim, general considerations of public feeling or public opinion (especially as interpreted by the media), or to judgments about the general character or prospects of the offender. The victim's situation and feelings should be recognised in other ways such as those indicated earlier in this chapter. Public feelings and public opinion can best be met by a careful explanation of the decisions which have been taken and by promoting a good general understanding of the principles involved. Attempts to improve the offender's character and prospects can properly be made within the context of a conviction and sentence properly imposed, but they should not determine the sentence itself. There is of course no justification for insulting and unfounded insinuations in cross-examination or pleas in mitigation, or insensitive remarks by judges when passing sentence. But it is difficult to see how it would be possible to promote Relational Justice by, eg relaxing the standard of proof for cases where the victim deserves special sympathy; imposing different sentences according to the victim's situation or feelings (or the way in which the victim described them to the court), or to the offender's general character or prospects (as they appeared to the court), or to the possible public reaction (because of the way in which a sentence might be reported in the newspapers), without also creating serious personal injustice. This is the tension between 'antiseptic' (or procedural) and 'passionate' justice which Jonathan Burnside discusses in *Chapter 3*. It is not easily resolved in the criminal justice system of England and Wales, where the present frustrations must be acknowledged but the traditional safeguards—such as the right to silence and the burden of proof—ought not to be lightly abandoned.

A radical new approach?

A more radical approach would be to question whether the process of arrest and prosecution is always the most suitable way of dealing with an offence or a suspect once he or she has been detected. There are many cases where the victim feels let down, even betrayed, by the process; or where it is not clear how the public interest has in any way been served. Examples include cases where the evidence proves insufficient to justify an arrest, where the prosecution is discontinued or abandoned or the defendant is acquitted on technical grounds; cases resulting (rightly or wrongly) in what is perceived as a trivial sentence; and cases which result in a relatively severe sentence but where the pain caused to the victim by the trial process, or the damage to the offender and his or her family, are out of proportion to any public interest which may have been served. It is possible for less serious cases of this kind to be dealt with by a police caution. The procedure has been criticised for 'trivialising' the offence and for allowing the offender to 'get away with it', especially if he or she is cautioned more than once; but cautioning can be successful if it is used in accordance with the principles of Relational Justice so that all relevant views are heard and the outcome is fully explained to all concerned.

A more ambitious scheme is the New Zealand 'Family Group Conference' described by Fred McElrea in *Chapter 7*. Comparable schemes exist in Australia, and a rather similar approach is adopted in relation to children's hearings in Scotland. There are also examples of mediation schemes in England, one of which was described in *The Guardian* newspaper on 25 August 1994. Nicola Baker explores further possibilities in *Chapter 5*. There are similarities with the idea of 'cautioning plus'—a police caution associated with an understanding that the offender will perform certain acts or take part in certain activities which will do something to repair the damage which has been done and help to keep the person out of trouble in the future.

The advantages of this approach are set out in *Chapter 5* and *Chapter 7*. But it would be foolish not to recognise the practical difficulties, and the possible objections of principle, which would be put forward if mediation or conferencing were too hastily adopted as a standard procedure in England and Wales. These would include:

- the difficulty in handling cases where the person denies the offence;
- the pressure which might be placed on a person to admit an offence which he or she has not committed;
- the relationship between the process of mediation and any proceedings in court—which might be thought to be compromised;
- complaints of injustice or lack of legitimacy if guilt is admitted and arrangements are entered into without the safeguards and authority of a court;
- the difficulty of enforcing any arrangements which do not have the authority of a court order;
- criticisms of inconsistency and unfairness if what are perceived as similar cases have different outcomes;
- the time and cost which effective mediation is likely to involve.

Supporters of mediation and conferencing will claim that these objections can be overcome, and they will point to the increasing interest in mediation which is now being shown in the family and civil courts.[11]

These are not arguments which can be resolved in this volume. But the issues, including the shortcomings of the existing procedures and the benefits which are claimed for an alternative approach, are clear enough to deserve serious attention. The benefits are likely to be greatest, and the objections easiest to overcome, in cases involving children. The government should publish a consultation paper setting out the issues and options, as a basis for serious and systematic discussion.

Conclusions and recommendations

To sum up—

(a) All services, institutions and professions involved in the criminal justice process should treat all those with whom they come into contact—in whatever situation or capacity—with courtesy, dignity and respect. This requirement should be reflected in mission statements and statements of purpose; it should be reinforced by measures of performance, where they are practicable, and by training and example; and work to carry forward the *Citizen's Charter* should cover the wider aspects of the relationships involved in the delivery of public services in the criminal justice field.

(b) The government, and other relevant organizations in the public and private sectors, should give serious attention to the recommendations of the independent working party set up by Victim Support to consider compensation for the victims of crime, and should prepare a programme for putting them into effect.

(c) The government and the Prison Service (including commercial companies that are running contracted-out prisons) should proceed energetically to implement in full the report by Lord Woolf and Judge Stephen Tumim on the prison disturbances in April 1990, and should consider further reforms which could be introduced in the same spirit.

(d) The Probation Service should emphasise the importance of holding offenders to account for the offences they have committed and of confronting offending behaviour, and of recognising and responding to the situations and feelings of victims. It should also do so in a context which lays stress on its own accountability and legitimacy. Courts should impose community sentences rather than sentences of imprisonment wherever it is possible to do so.

(e) The government should recognise the potential contribution and importance of networks of concerned citizens in measures to prevent crime and prevent re-offending, and should consider how they could most effectively be encouraged and sustained.

(f) Reforms of the police should be implemented, and the proposed new powers should be exercised, in a spirit which acknowledges the relational aspects of all police work, and the importance of the service's role in preventing crime and supporting communities as well as its role in law enforcement.

(g) Courts should be more accessible and locally accountable. They should have a stronger local identity, with more local involvement and more public discussion of their functioning and organisation. The government and the courts themselves should give serious consideration to the suggestions which are made in *Chapter 6* of this work, and the *Courts Charter* should be strengthened to take them into account.

(h) The Government should publish a consultation paper setting out the issues and options involved in family group conferencing, and the forms of mediation and reparation, as described in *Chapter 5* and *Chapter 7*.

Notes

[1] J Braithwaite, *Crime, Shame and Reintegration* (Cambridge: Cambridge University Press 1989).

[2] *Victim's Charter*: 'A Statement of the Rights of Victims of Crime' (London: HMSO 1990).

[3] *The Citizen's Charter:* (London: HMSO 1991).

[4] P. Rock, 'Governments, Victims and Policies in Two Countries.' *British Journal of Criminology*. 28/1 pp. 44-66.

[5] *'Compensating the Victims of Crime.'* Report of an Independent Working Party. (London: Victim Support 1993)

[6] Rt Hon Lord Justice Woolf, *Prison Disturbances April 1990: Report of an Inquiry,* (Parts I and II and His Honour Judge Stephen Tumim Part II), Cm 1456, (London: HMSO, 1991).

[7] *Custody, Care and Justice: The Way Ahead for the Prison Service in England and Wales,* Cm 1647, (London: HMSO 1991).

[8] J McGuire, *Offending Behaviour: Skills and Strategems for Going Straight* (London: Batsford 1985).

[9] A Bottoms, forthcoming

[10] D Faulkner, *The Guardian* 11 November 1993. Also *Strategic Government,* Spring 1994, 2/1, (London, ACC Publications).

[11] Sir Thomas Bingham, Address to the Annual General Meeting of JUSTICE (1994).

THE 'WOOLF REPORT': RECOMMENDATIONS AND PROPOSALS

Below are summarised the main recommendations and proposals of the report 'Prison Disturbances April 1990' by the Rt Hon Lord Justice Woolf and His Honour Judge Stephen Tumim:

We recommend:

1 Closer co-operation between the different parts of the Criminal Justice System. For this purpose a national forum and local committees should be established;

2 More visible leadership of the Prison Service by a Director General who is and is seen to be the operational head and in day to day charge of the Service. To achieve this there should be a published 'compact' or 'contract' given by Ministers to the Director General of the Prison Service, who should be responsible for the performance of that 'contract' and publicly answerable for the day to day operations of the Prison Service;

3 Increased delegation of responsibility to Governors of establishments;

4 An enhanced role for prison officers;

5 A 'compact' or 'contract' for each prisoner setting out the prisoner's expectations and responsibilities in the prison in which he or she is held;

6 A national system of Accredited Standards, with which, in time, each prison establishment would be required to comply;

7 A new Prison Rule that no establishment should hold more prisoners than is provided for in its certified normal level of accommodation, with provisions for Parliament to be informed if exceptionally there is to be a material departure from that rule;

8 A public commitment from Ministers setting a timetable to provide access to sanitation for all inmates at the earliest practicable date not later than February 1996;

9 Better prospects for prisoners to maintain their links with families and the community through more visits and home leaves and through being located in community prisons as near to their homes as possible;

10 A division of prison establishments into small and more manageable and secure units;

11 A separate statement of purpose, separate conditions and generally lower security categorisation for remand prisoners;

12 Improved standards of justice within prisons involving the giving of reasons to a prisoner for any decision which materially and adversely affects him; a grievance procedure and disciplinary proceedings which ensure that the Governor deals with most matters under his present powers; relieving Boards of Visitors of their adjudicatory role; and providing for final access to an independent Complaints Adjudicator.

Further reading

Allot P, *Eunomia: A New Order for a New World* (Oxford: Oxford University Press, 1990)

Beetham D, *The Legitimation of Power* (London: Macmillan, 1991)

Bottoms A E and Preston R H (Eds), *The Coming Penal Crisis: A Criminological and Theological Exploration* (Edinburgh: Scottish Academic Press, 1980)

Bottoms A E, forthcoming work on Intermediate Treatment

Braithwaite J, *Crime, Shame and Re-integration* (Cambridge: Cambridge University Press, 1989)

Coyle A, The Prisons We Deserve (London: Harper Collins, 1994)

Farrington D P and West D J, *The Cambridge study in delinquent development: a long-term follow-up of 411 London males, in Kriminalitat* (Berlin: Springer-Verlag, 1990)

Hauerwas S, *A Community of Character* (London: University of Notre Dame Press, 1981)

Home Office, *Custody, Care and Justice: The Way Ahead for the Prison Service in England and Wales* (London: HMSO, Cm 1647, 1991)

Jubilee Policy Group, *Relational Justice: A reform dynamic for criminal justice* (Cambridge: Jubilee Policy Group, 1994)

Kaye B N and Wenham G J, *Law, Morality and the Bible* (Leicester, Inter-Varsity Press, 1978)

MacIntyre A, *Whose Justice? Whose Rationality?* (London, Duckworth, 1988)

Marshall T and Merry S, *Crime and Accountability: Victim/Offender Mediation in Practice* (London: HMSO, 1990)

McElrea F W M, 'A New Model of Justice' in Brown B J and McElrea F W M, *The Youth Court in New Zealand: A New Model of Justice*(Legal Research Foundation, Auckland, 1993)

Sampson R J and Laub, J H, *Crime in the Making* (Cambridge, Mass: Harvard University Press, 1993)

Schacht J, *An Introduction to Islamic Law*(Oxford: Clarendon Press, 1964)

Schluter M and Lee D, *The R-Factor* (London, Hodder and Stoughton, 1993)

Shaw R, *Prisoners' Children: What are the issues?* (London: Routledge, 1992)

Stern V, Bricks of Shame (London, Penguin 1989)

Transcript of the Third Lincoln Conference, Relationships in Prison, April 1993. Copies available from The Bishop of Lincoln, Bishop's House, Eastgate, Lincoln LN2 1QQ

Tyler T R, *Why People Obey the Law* (New Haven: Yale University Press, 1990)

Victim Support, Report of an Independent Working Party, *Compensating the Victims of Crime* (London: Victim Support, 1993)

Wood C, *The End of Punishment. Christian Perspectives on the Crisis in Criminal Justice* (Edinburgh: Saint Andrew Press, 1991)

Woolf, Rt Hon Lord Justice, *Prison Disturbances April 1990* (Report of an Inquiry: Parts I and II and Tumim, His Honour Judge Stephen: Part II, 1991). (London: HMSO, Cm 1456)

Zehr H, *Changing Lenses* (Scottdale, Pennnsylvania: Herald Press, 1990)

Index

Z

Waterside Press titles include

Bail: The Law, Best Practice and The Debate Paul Cavadino and Bryan Gibson ISBN 1 872 870 11 2 £14.00 + £1.50 p&p. Contains an outline of the subject, comment, statutory provisions and case law. Suitable for practitioners and students. 'Highly recommended': *Justice of the Peace.*

Paying Back: Twenty Years of Community Service Edited by Dick Whitfield and David Scott. Foreword by Lord Taylor, Lord Chief Justice. ISBN 1 872 870 13 9 £12.00 + £1.50 p&p. Historical, analytical and with an eye to the future. Of interest to all practitioners, students and researchers. Good reviews across-the-board.

Drinking and Driving: A Decade of Development Jonathan Black. Contributions on Rehabilitation Courses by John Cook and John Martin. ISBN 1 872 870 12 0 £14.00 + £1.50 p&p. The law and practice of drink-driving. For lawyers, police and other practitioners. Includes useful checklists. 'Strongly recommended': *Justice of the Peace.* 'Invaluable': *Criminal Law Solicitors Association Newsletter*

Growing Out of Crime: The New Era Andrew Rutherford ISBN 1 872 870 06 6. £12.50 + £1.50 p&p. Second edition now reprinted. The classic work for everyone connected to the youth court. 'A brave book': *The Magistrate.*

Criminal Justice in Transition Bryan Gibson *et al* ISBN 1 872 870 20 1 £15.00 + £1.50 p&p. The second edition of the successful *Introduction to the Criminal Justice Act 1991.* An up to date account of sentencing law including the effects of the Criminal Justice Act 1993 and the Criminal Justice and Public Order Bill of 1994. With relevant statutory provisions and case references. Suitable for lawyers, other criminal justice practitioners and students.

The Youth Court One Year Onwards Bryan Gibson *et al* ISBN 1 872 870 14 7 £15.00 + £1.50 p&p. The second edition of the successful work *The Youth Court.* An updated treatment of the relevant law. Suitable for lawyers, youth justice practitioners and students.

Materials on the Criminal Justice Act 1991 Andrew Ashworth *et al.* ISBN 1 872 870 07 4 £12.00 + £1.50 p&p. All the supplementary information, materials and law arising between Royal Assent and implementation of the 1991 Act in October 1992.

Introduction to the Magistrates' Court Bryan Gibson ISBN 1 872 870 01 5 £7.25 + £1.50 p&p. An easy to read introduction for new JPs, practitioners and students. Contains a 500 word *Glossary of Words, Phrases and Abbreviations*. 'An ideal introduction': *Law Society Gazette*.

Punishments of Former Days Ernest Pettifer ISBN 1 872 870 05 8. £9.00 + £1.50 p&p. The history of punishments from the 18th century to modern times. 'A good read': *The Magistrate*.

Criminal Justice and the Pursuit of Decency Andrew Rutherford. Foreword by Lord Scarman. ISBN 1 872 870 21 X £12 + £1.50 p&p. Extracts from interviews together with a linking commentary examining the forces which drive a selection of senior criminal justice practitioners. Originally published by Oxford University Press. 'A highly readable and illuminating work': *Times Higher Education Supplement*.

Introduction to the Criminal Justice Process Paul Cavadino and Bryan Gibson ISBN 1 872 870 09 0 £12.00 + £1.50 p&p. Builds on the successful format of *Introduction to the Magistrates' Court* above (in preparation as at November 1994).

An Introduction to the Probation Service Anthony Osler ISBN 1 872 870 19 8 £12.00 + £1.50 p&p. An outline of the topic for newcomers of all kinds (in preparation as at November 1994).

An Encyclopaedia of Criminal Justice Julia Fionda and Andrew Rutherford ISBN 1 872 870 10 4 £19.00 + £1.50 p&p. (in preparation as at November 1994).

Bogus Law Reports Bryan Gibson ISBN 1 872 870 08 2 £9.00 + £1.50 p&p. A unique collection of fictional law reports. Spurious quotes, dubious principles and fragile arguments. 'A major new work': *The Justices' Clerk*.

Judicial Guidance on Sentencing Paul Cavadino (Details available on request).

Waterside Press, Domum Road, Winchester SO23 9NN Tel or fax 0962 855567. *Cheques should be made out to 'Waterside Press'. Organisations can be invoiced for two or more books.*

Relational Justice
Repairing the Breach

WATERSIDE PRESS
WINCHESTER